JUMPING
OFF
the
HAMSTER
WHEEL

**HOW TO RUN YOUR BUSINESS
SO YOU SLEEP AT NIGHT**

JAMIE CUNNINGHAM

Colin,
Make your Mark.
Jamie

IMPACT PRESS

First published in 2019 by Impact Press
an imprint of Ventura Press
PO Box 780, Edgecliff NSW 2027 Australia
www.impactpress.com.au

10 9 8 7 6 5 4 3 2

ISBN: 978-1-920727-36-9 (paperback)
ISBN: 978-1-920727-35-2 (ebook)

 A catalogue record for this
book is available from the
National Library of Australia

Cover and internal design by Deborah Parry Graphics
Printed and bound in Australia by Griffin Press of Ovato Book Printing

CONTENTS

FOREWORD

BY CHRIS CUFFE

Running a small business is not for the faint at heart. You are likely working long hours and even when you are not physically in your business, you are probably still mentally putting in hours. You likely have minimal resources in terms of people and money. And yet you still need to get as much done as a big business – but that big business has more resources, capability and hands to see it through.

It's no wonder that the failure rate of small businesses is so high. In my business experiences, even large organisations who have all the benefit of time on their side still have trouble getting it all done. With all that business owners are asked to keep on their plate, it's no wonder that incidence of anxiety and depression in the small business community is double that of the general population.

This book changes all that.

In the roughly fifteen years I have known Jamie Cunningham, I have witnessed his keen ability to guide business owners with those limited resources and help them be more savvy, more resourceful and act in smarter ways than their big business counterparts. Best of all, he helps them do it under their own power.

As a business owner, you do have an advantage over big business – agility. The agility to make changes and to morph your business to suit the market and your goals. With the right advice, it can be like having the wind at your back, and in small businesses that is a very good place to be.

However, to be able to use that advantage, you need to think strategically, which means not letting yourself get caught up in the day-to-day running of your business as most small business owners do. Most never escape the time trap, or as Jamie puts it, 'the Hamster Wheel', and spend their whole career trying to keep up. It's an exhausting prospect for business owners who have brilliant ideas and the right entrepreneurial mindset but just need a little help to execute.

This book gives you the resources to claim back your time and puts you in a position to think strategically and take advantage of your agility. Congratulations on picking this book up. Reading it, and using the tools within, will help you make the changes that will give you the business you deserve. So go out there and get it.

INTRODUCTION

WHAT IS THE
HAMSTER WHEEL?

EVEN IF you've never owned a hamster, it's not difficult to visualise the way they run on the stationary wheels in their cage. Their little legs are going crazy, yet no matter how much energy they put into it, they are going nowhere.

It's the same for many business owners. You have a powerful desire to move forward, grow your business and achieve some level of freedom and control of your life, yet no matter how tirelessly you work, the more time and effort you put in, the more you feel trapped and a slave to the very business you created.

No doubt, when you started your business, you had visions of grandeur. Writing your own future, being your own boss, making good money, adding value to the marketplace and, most of all, being in control of your own time.

The business hamster wheel is getting caught in the trap of doing so many things in your business that there aren't enough hours in the day to get it all done. And, because there is so much to get done, some of the most important things that will help grow your business – and afford you the freedom you signed up for – just don't get your attention. This applies to a large majority of business owners – maybe even you.

Even if your business is growing, you may find you're unable to extract yourself from underneath the multitude of functions you are so good at (and needed to be good at to get it growing in the first place), so that you are now working harder than your employees. The thought of a holiday, no matter how much you know you need one, induces stress, knowing things will fall apart the moment you step away for an extended period. So, the question begs, 'How do you get off the hamster wheel?'

Well, that's the premise of this book. I've pulled together the methodology I've been using since 2005 to help business owners achieve growth in a way that gives them the level of freedom they dream of – and a business that is strong, healthy and sustainable.

If you're reading this book, there are likely to be aspects of your business that you are not happy with, or challenges you would like to overcome.

First, rest assured you are not alone. Although it's not talked about very often, most business owners have aspects of their business they are not happy with. Whether it is financial, employee related or the lack of balance in their lives, you won't need to go far to find someone with a challenge they don't know how to solve that is causing them stress.

If we look at it, the only reason you have challenges is because you don't know how to solve them. Otherwise, they wouldn't be challenges! And the only reason you don't know how to solve them is because you don't have the knowledge to do so. This leads us to the conclusion that to overcome a challenge, you need knowledge.

There are three ways to gain the necessary knowledge. You can:

1. learn through trial and error (the slowest and most expensive approach, yet surprisingly common one for most business owners)
2. get advice (the fastest but also expensive, especially if you need to pay for that advice)
3. learn by reading and watching educational content (middle of the road for speed but probably cheaper than the other two options).

As humans, we are constantly learning through trial and error, but we don't need to learn *everything* this way because there are smarter ways to learn.

So, while I won't be so arrogant as to suggest this book is the only business book you need to read, I will say it's a great starting point. What I've outlined in the following pages represents the core principles and methodologies you need to know to be able to grow a successful, sustainable business and begin to get the results you want. By a successful, sustainable business, I mean a business that is growing, generating adequate free cash flow and giving you a level of time freedom that lets you experience the life you thought you would have when you started your business in the first place.

If you went to a library or bookstore, or searched online, you could find volumes of publications and articles dedicated to each of the topics this book covers. There are times when detail and depth are critical, and there are times when less is more. This book will not always go into the deepest level of detail, and that is for one simple and very important reason – as a business owner, you need to understand the whole picture and the core concepts surrounding each of the key areas of your business. When you understand things at that level, you can then more accurately assess where you need to shift your focus. That is the time when further detail will be valuable. This book is about giving you the 20 per cent of information that will enable you to get 80 per cent of the results, and it's about presenting the information in a way that shows you the map and how all the pieces fit together. It's not the be-all-and-end-all volume that comprises all you will ever need to read or learn. Learning never stops. This book will provide you with the context and the direction of where to focus your future learning efforts.

We can't all be experts in every area, so once you have a handle on the complete overview of all four core areas (presented in this book as the Four Keys), you can quickly assess where you need to dive deeper into your education, where you need to bring in experts, or where you need to delegate or outsource. Having this base knowledge allows you to effectively delegate and outsource because you know how things should work – at least at a base level.

Delegating or outsourcing an area of your business without a base knowledge of what you are delegating is business suicide. It's impossible for you to know if it's being done correctly or if the information you are being told is accurate. Never solely rely on the expertise of others – including me.

Just because I've written something in this book does not mean it's the only way of doing things. Your aim as a reader is to marry what you learn here with concepts you have discovered during your previous learning and experience. The main point is to critically question how any new idea would work within the scope of your business. Einstein himself insisted that, 'The important thing is not to stop questioning.'

That said, everything I've written in this book I practise myself in each of my businesses. It's the same content I use with my mentor clients, which represents the best practice and success from nearly 15 years of work. I truly hope you enjoy it, and more importantly, produce impressive results from implementing the strategies and concepts shared.

HOW TO USE THIS BOOK

First, the good news: you don't need to read this entire book to benefit from it. And what's more, I would probably advise that you *not* read the whole thing.

The reality is that most books that are bought are never read, and most books that are started are never finished. So really, most books do not have the effect their authors intended. The way I see it, if you can just read the parts that you are interested in, or are relevant to your situation, then a book is going to be of way more value. You can always come back for more when you are ready, have the time or your needs change.

The irony of growing your business is that while you can always benefit from useful information and growing your knowledge, you rarely feel like you have the time to do so. I mean, let's face it, you have a business to run, right?

In the following decision trees, I've outlined a few different problems and desired outcomes common to many business owners. The decision trees will help you to know where to start reading. They are important because often what people think they need is not always the right starting point. It's sometimes a case of not knowing what you don't know, so being guided by these decision trees will give you the best results.

Of course, reading the book from beginning to end is fine too. Even if there is an area you feel you are doing well in, no doubt you can still benefit, especially when you experience the topic from a new source or from a different viewpoint. These are tried-and-true methods presented in a unique way, which will allow you to find precisely what you need to fuel your business growth.

DECISION TREE #1

CASH-FLOW PROBLEMS?

Are you profitable?

YES → Read:
• Maximising and managing cash flow

NO → See **Decision Tree #2**

Must-read first principles
• #1 – It's all *you*, baby
• #4 – See your vision
• #7 – Planning brings clarity
• #8 – 80:20 Pareto principles

Other must-read sections
• Planning
• Execution and rhythm

DECISION TREE #2

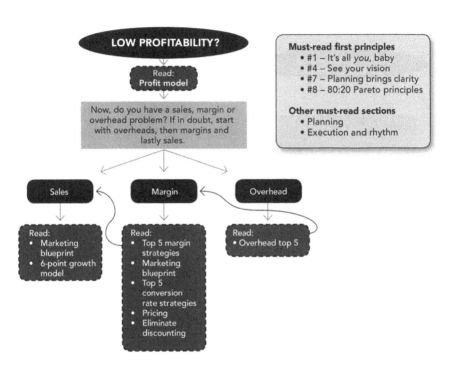

LOW PROFITABILITY?

Read:
Profit model

Now, do you have a sales, margin or overhead problem? If in doubt, start with overheads, then margins and lastly sales.

Must-read first principles
- #1 – It's all *you*, baby
- #4 – See your vision
- #7 – Planning brings clarity
- #8 – 80:20 Pareto principles

Other must-read sections
- Planning
- Execution and rhythm

Sales

Margin

Overhead

Read:
- Marketing blueprint
- 6-point growth model

Read:
- Top 5 margin strategies
- Marketing blueprint
- Top 5 conversion rate strategies
- Pricing
- Eliminate discounting

Read:
- Overhead top 5

DECISION TREE #3

SALES PLATEAUED OR DECLINING?

See **Decision Tree #2**
I know you think you have a sales problem, but first, let's be sure that is the root cause, then we'll grow your sales.

Must-read first principles
- #1 – It's all *you*, baby
- #4 – See your vision
- #7 – Planning brings clarity
- #8 – 80:20 Pareto principles

Other must-read sections
- Planning
- Execution and rhythm

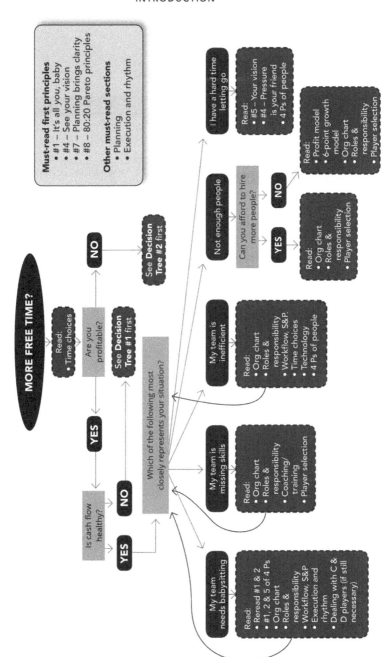

DECISION TREE #4

MORE FREE TIME?

Must-read first principles
- #1 – It's all you, baby
- #4 – See your vision
- #7 – Planning brings clarity
- #8 – 80:20 Pareto principles

Other must-read sections
- Planning
- Execution and rhythm

Read:
- Time choices

Are you profitable?
- NO → See Decision Tree #2 first

Is cash flow healthy?
- YES
- NO → See Decision Tree #1 first

Which of the following most closely represents your situation?

My team needs babysitting
Read:
- Reread #1 & 2
- #1, 2 & 5 of 4 Ps
- Org chart
- Roles & responsibility
- Workflow, S&P
- Execution and rhythm
- Dealing with C & D players (if still necessary)

My team is missing skills
Read:
- Org chart
- Roles & responsibility
- Coaching/training
- Player selection

My team is inefficient
Read:
- Org chart
- Roles & responsibility
- Workflow, S&P.
- Time choices
- Technology
- 4 Ps of people

Not enough people
Can you afford to hire more people?
- YES
Read:
- Org chart
- Roles & responsibility
- Player selection
- NO
Read:
- Profit model
- 6-point growth model
- Org chart
- Roles & responsibility
- Player selection

I have a hard time letting go
Read:
- #5 – Your vision
- #4 – Pressure is your friend
- 4 Ps of people

DECISION TREE #5

CAN'T FIND GOOD PEOPLE?

Must-read first principles
• #1 – It's all you, baby
• #2 – The respect matrix
• #5 – See your vision

Read:
• Org chart
• Roles & responsibilities
• 4 Ps – Purpose
• 4 Ps – Playing rules
• 4 Ps – Player selection

Other must-read sections
• Planning
• Execution and rhythm

DECISION TREE #6

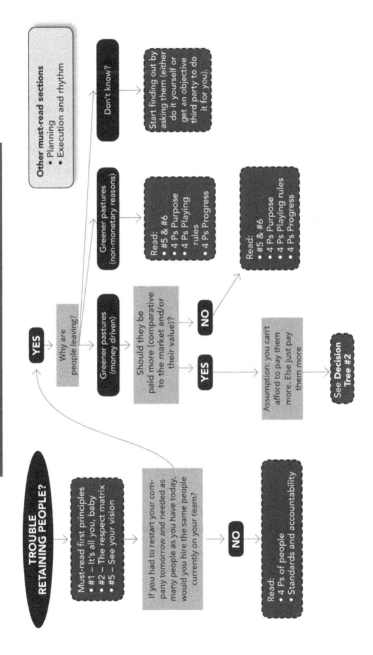

TROUBLE RETAINING PEOPLE?

Must-read first principles
- #1 – It's all you, baby
- #2 – The respect matrix
- #5 – See your vision

If you had to restart your company tomorrow and needed as many people as you have today, would you hire the same people currently on your team?

NO

Read:
- 4 Ps of people
- Standards and accountability

YES

Why are people leaving?

Greener pastures (money driven)

Should they be paid more (comparative to the market and/or their value)?

NO

Read:
- #5 & #6
- 4 Ps Purpose
- 4 Ps Playing rules
- 4 Ps Progress

YES

Assumption: you can't afford to pay them more. Else just pay them more

See **Decision Tree #2**

Greener pastures (non-monetary reasons)

Read:
- #5 & #6
- 4 Ps Purpose
- 4 Ps Playing rules
- 4 Ps Progress

Don't know?

Start finding out by asking them (either do it yourself or get an objective third party to do it for you).

Other must-read sections
- Planning
- Execution and rhythm

WHAT'S MY STORY?

Just to get things straight, I'm not a rags-to-riches story. I'm also not a youngster who has started 23 different companies and retired by the age of 27. I'm a regular person who puts their pants on one leg at a time. Yes, I've had financial success, which is essential, I suppose, if I'm writing a book on business – but I don't consider that to be my main point of credibility.

What I am proud of is the results I've created for others – those I've worked with formally and those I've influenced in passing. This book contains the toolbox and philosophies that I use in my businesses and with each of my clients. They are also philosophies I use in our family and my everyday life.

I've been coaching business owners since 2005, which came about quite by accident. In 2001, I was happily working in Sydney for my family business when my life path intersected with an incredible woman named Erin. One of the interesting points (of many) about Erin is that she is Canadian. This intrigued me, but as you can imagine, soon became inconvenient when her travels ended and she returned home to Canada.

Being one who never misses out on something I set my sights on, I promptly put a succession plan in place to extract myself from the family business and moved my life to Canada. After all, I had a girl to chase. Having had minimal experience in sales to this point, Erin was my first challenge. And given she is now my wife, I guess this was an early indication of my abilities!

After 10 years working hard in various roles throughout the family business, I found myself in Canada facing a
huge shift in employment. At university, I studied construction management. With my love of real-estate investing, I
thought I'd benefit from being in the construction game in
some capacity. Soon, the right role came along in Canada,
and I started working with a fellow named Steve. Steve was
a classic technician in the best kind of way. If you want
someone working on your house, you want Steve. He was
meticulous and his product was outstanding, but there was
a flip side. Steve knew very little about cash flow, profitability, hiring and managing people. So, while Steve was always
busy, things didn't always go according to plan, and as a
result, his business had hit a growth ceiling.

I didn't overthink my choice of work at the time, but
when winter rolled around, I knew I didn't want to be doing construction. Working construction during a Canadian
winter would strike fear into the heart of anyone with my
'Australian conditioning'. So I parted ways with Steve, and
my next adventure was working for Keith, who owned and
ran a small bicycle retail outlet – mountain biking happens
to be a huge passion of mine. It was while working with
Keith that I began to see a correlation between these two
businesses that was uncanny. Keith was having many of the
same problems as Steve, despite having considerably more
business acumen; was disorganised and just couldn't seem
to get it together. It was at this point that the light bulb went
on. I had an idea, which through naivety, I honestly thought
was unique. (I was 29 at the time.) I figured I should use
my strengths and expertise to help business owners improve
their business. Through some searching, I became aware of

an emerging field called 'business coaching'. I contacted a coach, who I bombarded with questions, and with very little due diligence, hung up my shingle as a self-declared business coach who could help anyone do anything. I didn't say that, but that is essentially what I was thinking.

Then, reality set in. I soon realised I had a lack of experience in sales and marketing, I was in a country where I knew virtually no one, and every business owner I talked to had never heard of a business coach. Cue the ominous music.

If it wasn't for the support of some key people in my life that year, I'm sure I would not be writing this book. But with this support, I threw myself into learning all I could and applying it like mad – to great results. Bit by bit, I had achieved success to the point where I brought on a business partner, and we hired other coaches to work with us. That little business was an incredible journey and far surpassed my expectations, *but it was the positive results that our clients were getting that fuelled me to continue the journey.*

The results went way beyond financials and growth metrics. Our clients were changing, their teams were changing, and the lens through which they now viewed the game of life was giving them scope to do extraordinary things.

As with all things, the time came for a change. Erin and I, with our growing family, were itching to move back to Australia. Since I'd set up my business in a way that I could effectively work from anywhere, we booked flights, packed up and headed off.

From a business perspective, our move back to Australia was interesting, to say the least. It gave me the opportunity to take all I'd learned in the past 10 years and apply it to a fresh market. However, as seems to be my style, we moved back to a part of Australia where I had zero connections. I was essentially starting from scratch, building my coaching business in this new market.

To do so, I applied all the principles written in this book. The business has once again grown beyond me, and we have a small but carefully selected team that embodies everything we stand for and everything we help our clients achieve.

The clients we work with span a multitude of industries across the globe, and our results have been noteworthy enough to ensure our business grows mostly through referrals and client loyalty. An important point worth noting: everything written in this book I work very hard to practise myself in each of our businesses. I say 'very hard' because I'm certainly not perfect. Outside of the coaching business, we are involved in various businesses and believe wholeheartedly in walking the talk. Being engaged with these businesses also means we are on the field playing the game, not sitting on the sidelines telling others how to play it. I think that is an important distinction.

My style of business is steady and consistent (which takes effort for me as it's not my natural style, but I believe it's the smartest way to grow a business). While I aim high, I'm a believer that many small steps can add up to massive results. I certainly didn't achieve success because of one or two 'big plays', but rather lots of little plays that have compounded over time.

The business world is filled with gurus advocating exponential growth and opportunities to 10x your business in record time. I believe in the power of big thinking, and I also see the delusion it can create when not approached well. Sure, there are stories of those who have built billion-dollar companies in fewer than 10 years, but they are the exception, not the rule. There is also a longer list of those who have tried and failed. As a mentor of mine, Keith Cunningham (no relation), says: 'Only an idiot plans their success by following the exception.'

(*Note*: I'll expand on big thinking later in the book. I'll share how to use it and how to avoid its potential sabotaging effects.)

I would be remiss if I didn't mention what I consider to be my biggest success – yes, I know it sounds corny … but it's true – is my amazing family. My wife Erin is incredible in so many ways, and my two beautiful kids, Kate and Lexi, give me an amazing amount of joy. For those of you who are lucky enough to have a close family, you'll know what I'm talking about. It might be a bit much to call it a success, as I'm only a part of the equation, but that is certainly the way it feels. And our fifth family member is Buddy, a tricoloured border collie, who is one heck of a dog. He is also amazing (most of the time).

Outside of family and business, I love the outdoors, particularly mountain biking, and I will never, ever, turn down the opportunity for a ride. We are very fortunate to live in a beautiful part of Australia – Beechworth, Victoria. It's an outdoor adventure playground. Like most things in our life, moving here was very intentional and fits 100 per cent with the philosophies I share in this book.

So that's me in a nutshell, folks. That's my story and I'm sticking to it.

FIRST PRINCIPLES

WHAT ARE
FIRST PRINCIPLES?

THE FIRST PRINCIPLES of business are like the *x* in an algebra equation. You won't be able to successfully solve the problem unless you know what the value of *x* is. They are the principles that underpin all events and circumstances that you will need to navigate your path to growing your business.

Consider gravity. It just exists. Barring a few specialised occupations, we don't need to know why or how it exists daily; we just need to know that it does. What would happen if you decided gravity didn't exist? Well, you would stop making decisions that take that very fact into account, which could lead to some disastrous consequences. The next time you parked on an incline, you wouldn't apply the handbrake of your car, and it would go careering downwards, leaving a path of destruction in your wake. Or, you wouldn't be concerned about stepping off the edge of a cliff – likewise, not a good outcome. I'm sure you get the idea.

Gravity is an obvious example because the consequences are so obvious, and we've been trained to understand it since we were born. Well, there are many other First Principles that we may or may not have been educated on but are similarly affecting the outcomes of our actions. Knowing them means knowing the laws that govern our business growth and, therefore, our lives. It's a game changer.

If you've read any self-improvement books, some of what I'm about to cover here may not be new to you, which is great. You see, the great (and surprising) thing about First Principles is that we are always working on a new level of mastering them. There is no level you reach where you'll be able to say, 'Yep, I know all I need to know about that one!' They are not the kind of thing you just check off or read a couple of times and forget about.

The importance of First Principles is not whether you've heard of them before, it's how well you're applying them or, better yet, how well you can explain them to someone else in a way that they immediately get.

Be careful about confusing principles with tactics. Tactics are the *how* to do something and principles are the *what* is going on. Once you understand what is going on, you can then choose the right how you are going to use. If you move to the how before understanding the what, you can often run around in circles, never reaching the outcome you desire.

You don't need to look far to see there are thousands of tactics out there. Tactics are in oversupply, causing many business owners confusion and, ultimately, stalled growth. And while tactics are many, principles are few. Those who know the principles and guide their decisions by them are more grounded, confident and their results show it. They don't need to consider the thousands of tactics because knowing the principles at play allows them to discard most tactics and narrow in on the few that are truly applicable to the situation.

Using and applying First Principles, however, can sometimes be easier said than done. It can require us to take a path that seems a little harder at times and may even require a bit of faith in the principle you are basing your decision on.

Following the First Principles is the difference between smarts and wisdom. It's the classic turtle versus hare scenario – knowing that sometimes the longest way really is the shortest.

In this book, I've chosen to include eight First Principles. Of all the principles we use with our clients, I consider them to be the most important and powerful. I've used my own language in describing them, but the concepts are certainly not mine. This is of key importance. Not every success needs to begin with a never-before-seen, radical concept. In business practice, there are several ways to bend the tried and true methods to fit your individual needs.

As you read this section, take some notes and spend a few moments after each principle to reflect on the question, 'How well am I doing on that one?'

Let's dive in.

RADICAL RESPONSIBILITY
– IT'S ALL *YOU*, BABY!

Yep, that's right – no one else but you. If you've been around for a while, this concept may not be new to you, but still, I challenge you on how well you live it. What I'm talking about here is taking radical responsibility for everything that goes on in your business and your life.

When I say, radical responsibility to attendees at a speaking engagement, most people nod their heads and say 'absolutely', yet when they start telling me about their business challenges, I can see they don't completely get it.

Most of us have grown up to understand responsibility as meaning someone can be trusted. What comes to mind for you when I say, 'John is a responsible person'? Most people would say, 'I can trust that John will make the right decisions.'

My definition of radical responsibility is:

No matter what happens in your business or your life, you are responsible for the outcome, because you choose how you will respond to events.

I've intentionally worded that definition in very blunt and bold terms. The way I see it, there are no grey areas. The word responsibility is made up of two words – 'response' and 'ability'. Put another way, responsibility is the ability to respond. So, in some ways, our interpretation of the statement concerning John would be correct. I see a problem, though with the word 'right', in 'right decision'.

You see, right is just a judgement based on a person's perception and is not relevant in defining the word responsibility. It's more of a moral issue and is subjective.

The true essence of responsibility is the awareness, ownership and commitment to the *fact* that we *always* have a choice in how we respond at *any* moment to *any* event.

The outcome of an event is not caused by the event; it's caused by our response to that event. The options available to us regarding how we respond are unlimited. It could be an action you take or simply an attitude you adopt. You are never pinned into a corner without choice. Any time you feel that way, you are simply avoiding radical responsibility.

In fact, most of us are blind to the choices available because of our conditioning, habits and patterns of thinking. Our responses are usually more accurately described as reactions, not responses. A response infers we have thought about what our next step is going to be; a reaction suggests it's something we just do without thinking.

The stories we tell ourselves about events and the subsequent meaning we give them largely drives our responses to the events we experience. We each have a set of beliefs about the way things are that we've developed over time. These beliefs shape the meanings we create and, in return, drive our responses. Realising that your beliefs and stories are just that, 'stories', is the first step. Separate them from fact and you can start to see how much control you do have – albeit most of the time it may not feel that way (because of our subconscious programming).

No one enjoys looking at themselves and saying, 'I was responsible for that' – but that is exactly what I'm asking you to do, in **every** situation. If you truly want to grow your company, you need to understand and be willing to live by the principle that your responses create your outcomes. And you have 100 per cent control over your responses.

Let me give you a personal example, one you might relate to if you've got or had young kids. It was nearing the end of the day and my two girls, Kate and Lexi (aged seven and three respectively at the time), were emotionally not at their best (and as it turns out, neither was I). There was a bit of bickering and backchat going on as we were preparing for dinner after a full day. Nothing over the top, but enough to put everyone on edge.

I had asked Kate to get drinks ready for dinner. This required her to get glasses out of the cupboard, which Lexi's legs happened to be dangling in front of as she was sitting on the kitchen bench. Maybe you can see where this is going.

As Kate tried to force the cupboard open, Lexi braced her legs more and more, and the battle for supremacy began. I was standing right there and asked both girls to back away and take a breath, then we could discuss it. I started with a very calm tone and found myself repeating my request two more times with slightly escalating volume each time, which was met with no response from my girls; my words seemed to fuel their desire to win the contest. Finally, I found myself yelling at them to stop. Well, that sent Kate off in tears and Lexi proceeded to overpower my yell with screams of her own. (How can such small people make so much noise?)

So, here's the question for you. What was my mindset at that moment? Did I feel like I had to yell? Absolutely. I could see no other way of getting them to stop. What choice did I have, right? It would be fair to say, at that moment, I felt they *made me* yell, even though that couldn't be further from the truth.

This example is typical of how most of us live our lives. We operate largely on behavioural autopilot by responding automatically to the events we face. The concept of radical responsibility means acknowledging that no person or event is ever *making* you do anything. Your response is 100 per cent up to you.

At that moment with Kate and Lexi, I could have chosen to get down to Kate's level physically, hold her gently on the shoulder, make eye contact and ask her to look at me. I could have chosen to check my state and adjust it before addressing the girls.

If I had approached Kate in a calm but strong voice, it could have broken the determined trance she was in, and we could have had a very different outcome. However, my emotional state at the time did not allow for such rational thought. I suppose you could say I was also determined in that moment to get my way.

On the flipside, you may be thinking, 'Well, I understand and believe all that, *but*, when our supplier lets us down, that is out of our control, so that is different. Or, 'If my employees are unreliable, that is not my fault.'

And herein lies the gold. If you allow yourself to have situations that don't fit the definition that you are 100 per cent responsible for your outcomes, you will tend to give yourself the benefit of the doubt when things are not 100 per cent clear (because you are human).

Let's remove the subjectivity of situational responsibility and keep it simple. It's the path that leads to higher levels of thinking and creativity. Choosing to believe there are outcomes that are out of your control puts you in a place of being the passenger and not driver. To grow our companies and have the life we want means choosing to be the driver and taking radical responsibility and control *all the time*.

Here's one more example for you that might hit closer to home. Mike was the owner of a business brokering company. He had some challenges finding good people and asked to have a chat to see if I could help him.

As we discussed the problem, I asked Mike to give me some background and his experiences to date. Here is what he said.

Over the past couple of years, I've hired three different sales people. The first person looked and sounded great. But after three months he left to take another job. The second person again seemed to be a perfect fit. One of her first projects was to look at a business about three hours north. She went up there to check it out and never came back [to work].

I was starting to see a pattern.

'And the third?', I asked.

'He's actually been with me for about a year and a half.'

'That's great,' I added, thinking it was a massive improvement on the previous two.

'Not really,' Mike admitted. 'He hasn't made a sale yet.'

Mmm, that's also a problem.

During this debriefing, I was getting a good feel for Mike. His tone and body language as he described the three hires were very telling. So I asked Mike to pinpoint the commonality between all three of the hires. His immediate response?

'They were all incompetent.'

Clearly, another follow-up question was required, so I inquired, 'Okay, what else is consistent with these three hires?'

At this point, I'm looking at him – *hard*. His response was, 'Jamie, are you trying to tell me that I'm the problem?'

I said, 'Mike, how could you be the problem? I mean you only wrote the ad, did the interviewing, chose the candidate, on-boarded them, trained them (or not), inspired them (or not), compensated them, created the environment for them to work in and held them accountable (or not).'

Mike really wanted to place the blame outside of himself. This situation is not unique to Mike. Have you ever said to yourself or others, 'It's hard to find good people'?

If we want to look outside of ourselves for the solutions, it can often be a fool's errand. Wanting our environment or other people to change is simply a way of absolving ourselves of radical responsibility.

Have some fun replaying situations where you know you've chosen to be the passenger. There will always be times when this happens, no matter how hard you try. The goal is not to be perfect, but to always be practising.

You are not always going to be in a place mentally where it's easy to take control of your responses. Don't beat yourself up over it. Just recognise what has happened, acknowledge that you messed up and move on. That's it.

If I had to pick one thing from this book that will create the most change in your business and life, this principle would be it. And to take it a step further, if you choose to implement this principle as part of the culture of your company (more on this later), it could be an absolute game changer. Perhaps you already have. If that's the case, you know what I'm talking about.

THE RESPECT MATRIX

Zig Ziglar is famous for saying, 'You can have anything in life you want, if only you help enough other people get what they want.'

The concept of the Respect Matrix was introduced

to me when I first read Steven Covey's landmark book *The 7 habits of highly effective people.*

In Figure 1, you can see that the Respect Matrix is all about the types of outcomes people generate when working together. In the figure, there are four quadrants, and in any given situation where two or more people are working together, each is playing in one of the four quadrants. Which quadrant someone is in may depend on whose perspective you are viewing it from.

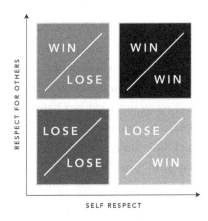

FIGURE 1: RESPECT MATRIX

In a competitive environment where you want to win, create a successful business and so on, it can be easy to be solely focused on winning. This can come at a cost. It can often blind you to what the other side needs. (When I say the other side, think about a relationship with a supplier or employee to give you some context.) If we are not allowing the other side to also win, we are slowly eroding goodwill and quality of relationships. And we need these relationships to be strong to win in the long game.

How long would you want to do business with someone who is always screwing you over and generating win/lose outcomes where you are the loser. No one is going to play that game for too long. Even if you feel you can get away with win/lose (where you are the winner) because the other person needs your business, there will come a time (and you don't know when it will be) when the scales balance out, and you will be the loser. This is just the way it works. Things always balance in the long run.

Knowing this, you might quickly realise the ideal quadrant to be in is the win/win quadrant; however, getting there is not always simple. Furthermore, we are not always aware of where we *choose* to play. We all have behavioural tendencies that may hinder us from naturally thinking win/win.

The reality is, many of us do play the win/lose or lose/win game. Sometimes, and perhaps more often than we realise, we play a game that's lose/lose.

In the figure, you can see the scales are both based on respect, which is the basis of win/win thinking. When respect drops, we start to get 'lose' outcomes in various quadrants.

Consider this scenario: you have a star employee (from a skill set and results point of view). The problem is, no one else in the company likes them because they are arrogant, they think they are above the rest of the team, and they play by their own rules. They are not a team player. Now you, as the business owner, are conflicted. You like the results this person brings in, but you realise they are making the rest of the team unsettled. What do you do?

Let me ask it a different way. Where are you playing on Figure 1 by having this person on the team? Of course, there are a variety of ways to look at this depending on whose perspective you are viewing it from, but I challenge you to justify this as a win/win situation. Often, I've seen business owners justify this person's existence, and it's usually done more out of fear than logic.

In every interaction, there is simply no need to settle for anything less than win/win. And if a win/win can't be reached, then you shouldn't be playing the game with each other. Find someone who does think in terms of win/win.

Of course, there are times when it makes sense to sacrifice a win to create a bigger win/win down the track. Just be honest with yourself about where you are choosing to play.

One of the biggest challenges with creating win/win outcomes is that it can take work. It's not always the obvious answer and often goes against common thinking. By work, I mean creative thinking and a willingness by both parties to work together. To get both parties to work together can take some communication magic. These are all skills that, when lacking, tempt us (and sometimes make it seem like the only available option) to settle for some form of a win/lose outcome.

Win/lose outcomes can look like either/or outcomes. If I want A and they want B, it appears we must choose one or the other, which means whoever doesn't get their choice must go without. This is usually a sign of lazy thinking. Instead, invest some time and challenge yourself to come up with the '*and*' solution. Meaning, how can you both have A and B? Here are some questions to guide you.

- For us to be willing to give the other party what they want, what would we need to have/know/feel/hear/believe?
- What would need to be different for us to get A and B?

- For the other side to be willing to give us A, what would they need to have/know/feel/hear/believe?
- What do we have now that we would be willing to give up to get A?
- What assumptions are we making about this negotiation? How can we validate/challenge these?
- What would the perfect outcome look like for this?

To draw upon a personal situation to illustrate the point, our family often finds itself with what seem like win/lose or even lose/lose outcomes when trying to work out what to do on weekends with the kids. Invariably, my wife and I have errands or tasks we want to get done, and the kids want to go somewhere and play.

When we feel pressured for time, the bully parent (me) will say something like, 'You guys need to understand these errands must get done. This is the way it has to be.' If that was the outcome, it would clearly be a win/lose situation (meaning the kids are not happy, which means the parents are also not happy, so it is potentially a lose/lose situation in the end).

The best outcomes are when we list who wants to do what and treat it like a jigsaw puzzle, moving all the pieces around until everyone is getting what they want. And the best part is, the kids work it out, not us.

The same concept can work in business. Get clear on what everyone wants and invest a bit of time looking at options. If a supplier needs to maintain a price, perhaps they'll give on terms. If an employee wants to start late, perhaps they can cover the phones when others have left for the day, and that gives you longer trading hours.

Be creative and adopt the mantra of the *and* solution versus the *either/or*.

A few other points to consider:

- Growing businesses requires strong relationships with others, and people like having relationships with those who care if they win.
- Helping other people to win is never about giving up what you want. Your needs are just as important as anyone else's. Getting what you want is critical. Never mistake lose/win for win/win when it is constantly putting other's needs ahead of your own.
- A win/win solution can always be found, but it rarely presents itself on a silver platter. More commonly, it requires hard work and creative thinking.
- A win/win solution requires all parties involved to be committed to finding one. You can have a massive influence on how others perceive the effort to find a win/win. Don't cop out as soon as someone appears to be more interested in win/lose. Be a leader.
- You can only find a win/win with someone who also wants a win/win. Contrary to the point above, also know when it's time to find someone else to play with.
- The final word (which may contradict all I've said on this point so far): not all situations warrant the time investment that may be necessary to find the win/win. If the consequences of win/lose or lose/win are minor, sometimes it can make sense just to get on with it. Invest the time where it matters most. Just be aware that where it matters most needs to be considered from everyone's perspective. Sometimes it can matter more to one party than the other, so be careful

of falling into the trap of thinking it's no big deal just because to you it isn't.

INPUT AFFECTS OUTPUT

Nothing comes from nothing. There are no free lunches, and the world owes you nothing. These are good words to remember in your quest for business growth.

A useful analogy is to think about a space shuttle. For a space shuttle to get into space, it requires massive amounts of energy. It needs to overcome the forces of gravity, and in doing so, burns an extraordinary amount of fuel.

The interesting thing is, most of the fuel that a space shuttle uses for its whole flight is used in the earliest stages of its journey. Only once it has reached space can much smaller amounts of fuel propel the spacecraft over great distances.

It's the same with business. The stage you are at in your business will determine how much fuel is required to achieve the desired growth rate. To sit back and think you can just do things smartly is usually a recipe for disaster. Smart is good, and working your ass off is commendable, but both smart and hardworking is much better.

Of course, in keeping with our space shuttle analogy, we do need to be smart in how we apply the fuel. A space shuttle has a flight plan and controls to help it stay on course. This is all in place before the fuel is ignited. In our business, we can't just blindly go and take massive action (apply fuel) without it being planned and directed. One of the key elements of this First Principle is to know how much input (action) is required to achieve our goals. And it's usually more than you think.

The input required is a function of where you are, relative to your desired goal, the amount of momentum you currently have and how fast you want your goal achieved. It's largely physics.

This principle will guide you to be realistic in your plans. For example, if you are looking to grow your business by 10 times in the next 3 years, hiring one extra sales person probably won't do the trick. There's a good chance you'll need to think and plan significantly bigger than that.

Another aspect of this principle is the law of critical mass. Critical mass states that desired output levels may not be seen until a certain level of inputs has been made. In addition to that, outputs are not always in direct proportion to inputs at the time the inputs are given. There often is a time lag.

For example, you may inject a lot of effort and activity into your marketing, but it can take some time to see the fruits of your labour. Be wary of stopping your efforts or changing to something new too soon before critical mass has had a chance to kick in.

Another strange but true element of this principle is that the output does not always come from the expected input. Have you ever done a favour for a friend, not expecting one in return, and then someone (unrelated) does something for you? We often see this in the context of marketing – you may execute a brilliant campaign only to have a massive opportunity present itself from somewhere completely unrelated to the campaign activity.

Now, I'm not suggesting that if a marketing activity is consistently not working directly, it's okay to keep doing it just because the activity alone might magically bring the results in from somewhere else. I am saying that if the activity is well planned and executed at the appropriate level of magnitude, results will come, but the path they take is not always predictable.

The key to this philosophy is to give inputs at the level that will enable you to achieve your goals, but not get caught up in where or when the results will flow. Just know they will. Faith and belief backed by action and patience make this principle work in your favour.

In conjunction with this, look for the signs that you are on the right path. Look for the feedback. Don't be in denial when the signs might be telling you otherwise.

PRESSURE IS YOUR FRIEND

In 1977, Ilya Prigogine received a Nobel Prize for his work in thermodynamics. From this work came the law of perturbation. This law states that for something to change state, both time and pressure is required.

Consider a diamond. It starts off as a piece of coal then, over time and with lots of pressure (from being deep within the earth), it changes state into a diamond. And a diamond is way more valuable than a chunk of coal. The same can be said for you and your business. For both to become more valuable, pressure over time is required.

Now, you might be saying, 'Jamie, I've got pressure. Pressure to meet payroll, pressure from my family to spend more time with them, pressure from employees to answer their questions. I don't need more pressure.' And yes, I'd agree with you; however, there are two kinds of pressure – reactive and proactive. *Reactive* pressure is put on you by forces outside of you; *proactive* pressure you put on yourself.

All those pressures of payroll, family and employees are usually reactive. You feel they are happening *to* you. The difference with proactive pressure is it's *your choice* to apply it.

Proactive pressure can and should feel like it's pulling you toward something great. When an athlete spends extra hours in the gym beyond what may be required, it's because they have a strong vision of what they want to achieve, and they feel driven to do the extra work.

The best form of proactive pressure comes from having a clear, compelling vision of what you want to create and knowing why you want to create it. When you can see and feel that goal – when you can taste it – it has a pulling effect that is a form of pressure. To think about it makes you feel inspired and motivated to act (see the First Principle: See your vision).

A lack of vision or clarity on meaningful goals means you are left to react to the environment around you. If there is no force or pressure (such as your vision or goals) pulling you forward, then you are left with pressure pushing you from behind. And that is the reactive pressure. Reactive pressure still serves a purpose because it gets you moving, however, the associated feelings are often not what you are looking for.

So, the true principle here is: 'Proactive pressure is your friend.'

To see how this is currently working for you, look at the different areas of your life: your health, relationships and finances. Odds are that you are proactive in at least one of these three. If you look deeper and ask why, you'll probably find it's because you have a vision or a standard you wish to maintain.

Which brings us to the second way to bring about proactive pressure – through your personal standards. Standards are simply the minimum you are willing to settle for. They are like the thermostat for that area of your life.

Take health, for instance. Everyone has a standard they are happy to maintain regarding diet and exercise. For some of us that standard seems almost non-existent, yet for others, it's clear the standard or personal benchmark has a hard line. Some people religiously train a minimum of 4 days per week, and if a week goes by where they don't exercise, they are determined to get back on track the next week. That is proactive pressure.

For your business to grow, you need to decide the minimum standard you are willing to settle for. What level are you going to make non-negotiable? Because whatever level you decide on will become your reality. Like I said, your standards are like your thermostat. Your growth will rise to that level.

So, you might be asking, 'If my standards determine my level of success, how do I change my standards?' To answer that, let's look at the next two principles.

SEE YOUR VISION

Simply stated, your vision is a picture of the future you want for yourself.

On a very simple level, you might be able to relate to a vision you had in which you wanted to secure a new client or star employee. In thinking about it before it happened, you may have pictured what it would be like, what the benefits would be and perhaps even how the conversation would go that would bring about the outcome (vision) you wanted.

Invariably, if we get clear on an outcome we want, and can see it in our mind's eye in a way that makes it look and feel real, that outcome has a very high probability of becoming our reality.

In the field of sports psychology, visioning is now a mainstream training method. Athletes are trained to visualise the goal they are striving for. In fact, the method has evolved beyond just visualisation to imagination. Visualising is the act of seeing with your mind's eye, but imagination involves all the senses.

Athletes are trained to imagine both the goal and the events leading up to the goal over and over in their mind until it becomes crystal clear. They do this to the point that playing it in their minds looks, feels and smells real. Every detail is accounted for: what they are wearing, whom they are competing against, what emotions they are feeling, what the crowd looks and sounds like, the smell of the track and so on.

When we take that same exercise and apply it to our business, it can have outstanding results. There can, of course, be some challenges in doing this activity. First, many people simply don't know what they want. More often they just know what they don't want, which thankfully can be a great start.

If this is you, here is a helpful exercise: grab a blank piece of paper and draw a vertical line down the centre to divide the page in two. In the left column, write down all those things you don't want. In the right column, write down the opposite of what you've put on the left.

For example, if you wrote in the left column 'all the debt I currently have', in the right column you might put 'consistent positive bank balance with strong free cash flow'.

It's easy to glance at this principle and think, yeah, that makes sense, then leave it at that. I've certainly made that mistake in the past. Yet I will stress, *a big reason that you may not have what you want is that you are not clear on what you want.* Please don't underestimate the importance of a clear and compelling vision. As I mentioned in the previous principle, your vision should be the thing that gives you enough emotional fuel to raise your standards and put positive pressure on yourself. If you are not clear on your vision, it leaves you vulnerable to mediocrity, procrastination and frustration over lack of progress.

There is also the challenge of 'how' you are going to make that vision come to reality. I have seen people give up on crafting a compelling vision because the belief of attaining it is weak, or they feel they just don't know how to do it. If this is you, it's okay to feel this way. And the good news is, this book contains the steps and how-tos required to build the business you imagine. Don't let those obstacles get in your way. Give yourself permission to dream and create the business and life you want, first in your mind, then as we progress through the book, in reality.

To help you create a vision for yourself, here's an excerpt from our 90-day planning tool (a tool we use with clients to keep them on track and be clear on where they are going and how they are going to get there).

(*Note*: you'll see this excerpt starts with the personal stuff. I suggest you start here because, at the end of the day, that is usually what is most important to you. Make sure the vision you create for your business serves and is aligned with the personal vision you have for *your* future.)

Creating long-term goals

The first step in creating your plan is to get some long-term perspective. Before you can map out the short term, you need to know where you want to end up in the long term. If you have never done this before, carve out some serious time to think this over. Perhaps sitting somewhere inspirational with a glass of wine (my preference) can do the trick. The environment you choose will help.

If you've already done plenty of long-term planning, you can move through this section a little faster, although it still pays to give it some thought. As our lives change, what is important can also change, and having a sense of what is important to you in the long run is critical to staying on track.

Allow yourself to dream here. It's not necessary to know how you are going to achieve these long-term goals. That will come later. The most important part is to start to get a sense of what you ideally want your life to look like. Use the following questions to guide you. Some of these questions are very deep, some not so much, but they are all intended to help you design your ideal life. Give yourself permission to be idealistic. Shut down the voice that tells you, 'That's not practical.'

Purpose-finding questions

1. If success was guaranteed, what would I choose to do?
2. If money and time were not limited, what would I do?
3. What am I good at?
4. What am I passionate about?

5. What does a legacy look like by my definition?
6. What would I have to do to create a legacy?
7. What do I enjoy doing the most?
8. How can I create the most value for people doing what I enjoy the most and am the best at?
9. How much impact can I have in the world? How would I do it?
10. If there were one global problem I would like to solve, what would it be?
11. If my mission was to have an impact on a billion people, how would I do it?

Lifestyle-defining questions

1. What would my ideal day look like?
2. What are the key activities I need to be engaged in to feel fulfilled?
3. Who are the people I like to be around to feel connected?
4. What would my ideal year look like?
   - How many hours am I working?
   - What do I do for vacation?
   - What do I do for enjoyment?
   - What do I do to fulfil my purpose?
5. Where do I want my income level to be?
6. What does my investment portfolio look like?
   - stocks
   - real estate
   - private company investments
   - insurance and fixed income
7. What experiences am I having?
8. How would I define the person I want to be? What is my future identity?

Business-defining questions

Now for your business. It's critical to acknowledge that business goals and personal goals can be closely linked (ie your passion and your fulfilment may come largely from your business activities). For some this will be true; for others, it may not be. The key question to ask yourself here is, 'For me to be able to enjoy my ideal life (as defined by the goals above), what does my business need to look like?'

1. What is my role in the business?
2. How many hours am I working?
3. What other key people will I need?
4. How big is the business?
5. How profitable will the business need to be?
6. What will operating cash flow need to be? (More on this later.)
7. How will the business need to be positioned in the market? (Major player, minor player, international market, local, etc.)
8. What will the succession/exit plan need to look like?

Looking at your answers to these questions, go ahead and establish some long-term business goals. As with the life goals, these are subject to change as you change – nothing is cast in stone. It is simply giving you a direction in which to start. Hopefully, once you invest some time in these questions, you can start to get a clear idea on what is important to you and what it might start to look like when it has been realised.

My personal experience with this principle is that my vision has evolved over time. There are some elements that have stayed consistent, but others that have changed. All the while, my vision has become increasingly clear over time. Today, my vision is many times clearer than it was 10 years ago. And I have no doubt it will continue to gain clarity.

If you are having trouble gaining any sense of certainty or clarity, give yourself permission to let it go for a while. If you understand and agree with the importance of the principle and have invested a fair amount of time in the previous questions, have faith that your vision will come to you over time. Don't be in a rush. Allow it to evolve.

YOUR ENVIRONMENT
MATTERS

If you are a smoker and want to stop smoking (ie you want to change your status to that of non-smoker), which of these two strategies would you recommend?

1. Use self-control and willpower.
2. Remove the influence altogether. Maybe find some new friends to hang around who don't smoke and will never offer you a cigarette. In fact, you know these new friends may even look down on you if you were to smoke (shame, despite its obvious negative associations, can be a powerful short-term motivator).

The choice is obvious. And, it may be some form or combination of the two. The important lesson here is your environment will affect your behaviour, your drive and your motivation.

The people you hang around matter. If you have standards you want to reset around growth (or any other part of your business or life for that matter), you will be well served to find others who share those standards and values. It does not mean you have to cut your existing peer group loose (although sometimes that can be a good thing), it's more about changing the allocation of time to each group. Changing the people you hang around does not always have to mean personal relationships. You can change who influences you by reading, listening to and watching other people. There are almost limitless choices and availability of fantastic content that can change your life and your business. And you can access it all with the click of a button.

Rather than watching the news and becoming depressed, watch a TED talk or search up motivational videos and be blown away. If motivational videos are not your thing, pick a topic you know you need to be better at, and search out some information on that topic. There is so much free stuff out there, and you can have it all.

Another key part of your environment is your physical environment. Much of our habits and ways of thinking are triggered subconsciously by what we see and hear all around us. So, being intentional about what goes into your brain through your sensors can be a game changer.

Let's say you're sitting in your office. Papers are piled up around you; curtains are drawn; there is very little fresh air; it's dark, dull and sterile; and your bare walls are painted a bland, lifeless colour. Your chair creaks and the adjustment levers are broken. The tap in the background is dripping and you can tell someone is outside smoking because you can hear them barking up a lung. Close your eyes and put yourself in that scene. How do you feel? Inspired? I'm guessing not.

Let's try a different example. Your office overlooks the ocean, there is a fresh breeze coming in and you've just returned to your desk after a brisk walk along the beach. Your office has simple but clean furniture and there are some pictures on the walls that motivate and inspire you. Next to your desk is your 90-day plan, and in the top drawer of your desk is a detailed description of the vision you have for your life and your business. On your bookshelf are a variety of business classics that you've enjoyed reading over the years. You have a conference call coming up with your mastermind group, which is comprised of people you respect and admire, and whom you know will challenge you to step up and be great. Now, close your eyes and picture that scenario, and once you have it, picture it in the context of the ideal business you are working to create. An office by the beach may not be your ideal, or not even suitable depending on your business, but you get the idea.

Having visualised these two different scenarios, put yourself in the shoes of someone looking to do business with you.

If these two scenarios existed, and the people in the offices described above were competitors who shared similar skill sets, background and abilities, and they were both asking you for an investment, who would you put your money on?

Of course, the second scenario is again a no-brainer. So, if this is true, how inspiring is your current physical environment? What changes could you make to have it better serve you? How might changing your environment help to raise your standards or create a shift in how you see yourself?

PLANNING BRINGS CLARITY

It's one thing to have a goal in mind, even to have it written down, but it's another thing altogether to do the thinking required to plan out how to make that goal a reality. Of course, planning does not always ensure success. We still need to execute our plan. In fact, even executing our plan doesn't ensure success either – so what exactly is the point of planning?

The act of planning gets your mind working at a level that just doesn't happen in day-to-day operations. It's very hard to think strategically and creatively when your environment is filled with in-the-moment actions and distractions.

Having a plan grounds and guides you in your day-to-day life in a way that creates focus and awareness of the high-priority items. Without that awareness, you will tend to drift and react like a windsock, going whichever way the day takes you.

Planning is the product of consciously organised thought. This discipline of conscious critical thinking helps to make goals real in your mind. When you put pen to paper and list out different ideas, strategies and tactics, you will start to see which options look the best, or even create new options that were not available to you prior to investing the time in planning.

Rather than list a whole planning methodology here, I'm going to point you to the companion resource centre (jumpingoffthewheel.com) for this book where you can access a video, workbook and templates that will guide you through how to create an executable plan.

I'll just mention a few key points for you to consider.

- Block out the time for planning in your calendar now. Allow a half or full day each quarter. (If that sounds like a lot of time to you, that's your indicator that you absolutely need it.)
- Make sure you do it off-site, in an environment different to your office.
- Get your key people involved. The more input they have, the more they will own the plan. You need that ownership mentality to make the plan successful.

80:20 PARETO PRINCIPLE

The universal 80:20 principle discovered by the economist Vilfredo Pareto is a game changer. This principle is quite well known but much less utilised.

The principle states that in most situations, 80 per cent of the outputs come from 20 per cent of the inputs. Some examples include:

- At a picnic, 80 per cent of the food will be eaten by 20 per cent of the people.
- Eighty per cent of your garden's crops will come from 20 per cent of the plants.
- Eighty per cent of your profits come from 20 per cent of your customers.
- Eighty per cent of complaints and problems come from 20 per cent of your customers (usually not the 20 per cent who are responsible for your profits).
- Eighty per cent of your results come from 20 per cent of your activities.

The list goes on. This principle is massively helpful when deciding how to invest resources (time or money).

For example, if you wanted to look for a quick way to boost profitability and efficiency, you would review what your 20 per cent most and least profitable products and services are. Odds are, the ones that are most profitable are the ones you are most efficient at, and the opposite would probably be true for the least profitable 20 per cent.

You could then ask, 'What would happen if we stopped doing our least profitable, and invested in marketing and promotion of our most profitable?'

This kind of simple analysis can lead to some powerful questions and insights. It helps you to look at your business in new, but effective, ways. Don't get too caught up in the exact number, however. Sometimes the ratio is 90:10 or even 95:5. It could even be 60:40. The point is, most of the outputs come from a minority of inputs. Your goal is to identify the minority of inputs to focus your resources on.

Here are some simple questions to include in your next planning session to better utilise this principle.

- Which 20 per cent of marketing activities bring our best results?
- If I had to stop doing 20 per cent of the tasks I currently do, what would I get rid of? (Think of skill set, enjoyment and stress to guide you here.)
- Who are our top 20 per cent customers and what are we doing to better nurture/service them?
- Who are our bottom 20 per cent customers and what actions might be required for them to take up less of our resources?

- Which small amount of expenses make up the bulk of our total expenses? What can we do to reduce them?

In writing this book, I am working to utilise the 80:20. This book could be much longer and have way more content, but I've attempted to cut out the 80 per cent of fluff and just give you the 20 per cent that will make the biggest difference. It should hopefully make this book more valuable to you.

WRAPPING UP THE FIRST PRINCIPLES

It's a good idea to revisit these First Principles from time to time. They are concepts that have many levels of understanding, and you will find as you move forward in your journey, they will have more and more meaning as you reflect on situations and look for the principles at play.

Be a student of them. Teach them to others. And when you get stuck, come back and ask which principles you might be able to draw upon to help overcome your obstacles.

THE THREE LEVELS
OF GROWTH

TO APPLY THE TOOLS and strategies you'll be learning in this book; it will be helpful for you to have some context on what type of business you are building. By 'type', I'm referring to what level of growth.

Every privately held business on the planet is in one of three stages of growth, which I call the driver, the pilot and the owner. These three stages represent the role of the owner within the business.

Below, I explain what each of these three levels looks like, what is good about each and what the common problems are at each level. Before I get into that, I want to point out one key thing – no stage is any better or worse than another. There is no right stage to be at or going for.

Every person is unique in their goals and what they want from their business.

In the world of business advice and business coaching, there is a message out there that you must be at the owner stage of business (ie a business that works without you). And while that is a worthy goal and there are lots of benefits, it's not the only goal.

In fact, I've seen countless successful businesses at both the driver and pilot stages. And like all stages, the driver and pilot have pros and cons. So, whatever stage you are at, or want to aspire to, the key focus should be building your business so it performs optimally at the stage you are at and being aware of the risk that stage brings. If you are at the driver stage and feel you should be aiming for the owner stage, but it doesn't really excite you, then let it go. Start by building an awesome driver business. Once you've done that, you can work out what the next stage should be. And now, in a seemingly contradictory statement, a business must always be growing. So, don't sit back and think that once you've got your business to a certain stage, you are done. *You are never done*.

That said, growing does not have to mean growing up a level (eg from pilot to owner), but it does mean growing in some way. This might be technology, innovation, better ways to solve problems, better ways to leverage and grow without adding people and so on. There are lots of options for growth. Perhaps replacing the word growth with improvement is a more accurate way to look at it.

You should also be thinking about what your business *needs to look like* to sell it down the road. Make no mistake, there will come a time when selling your business is the right decision for you, and for a business to be sellable, it needs to have certain characteristics.

Now, let's get into it and look at each level.

THE DRIVER

The driver stage is where most people start. And for many, they never move past this stage, which again is fine, depending on what you want. If you are at the driver level, *you are* the business. Usually, if the driver is not present in their business, the business is not running, or at least not for long. They may be a solopreneur or have a small team (usually less than seven). They are usually the key sales person and the person running operations.

The problems at driver level can look like this.

- Very time poor: with so many priorities and few people to delegate to, drivers often finds themselves working long hours and not always feeling a sense of progress.
- Tight cash flow: because they wear so many hats, often they cannot (or are not sure how to) get the marketing engine running at full hum, the consequences of which are that the work can be feast or famine. Financial systems are also usually incomplete or lacking, so they are really flying by the seat of their pants.
- Stressed: the above two points over time can lead to excess stress, and eventually, burnout. Drivers in this state can keep it going for a while, but eventually, the tank hits empty and they don't have the reserves to keep going.

When it's going well for the driver, it may look like this (depending on the business, industry and goals of the owner):

- healthy cash flow and profitability that allows the owner to have some excess cash to invest

- ability to have some time off, but not long, extended breaks (typically one, maybe two weeks at a time)
- elevated levels of agility – you can make strategic changes very fast
- peaks and valleys of workload that may impact on you, the driver, directly from a time and stress point of view because you don't have the depth of capacity (people) to level out peak loads of inbound work
- strong protection against loss of customers due to loss of key people because it's you who holds most of the relationships with your customers.

Common thoughts at this stage include:
- 'If only I could just find someone like me, I'd be set.'
- 'It's hard to get it *all* done.'
- 'I just need a week of uninterrupted time, and I'd be all caught up.'
- 'I can't afford to hire the people I need.'

THE PILOT

The pilot has a team that can do most of the work that the driver must do themself. However, the pilot is still very much engaged in the day-to-day by making sure the cogs are greased and things are running smoothly.

When it comes to sales, the pilot may (and usually does) have others helping with sales, but they may still be the sales leader. (Most people call the person running the sales department the sales manager, but I call them the sales leader or sales coach because my belief is that a manager manages resources and a leader leads people. I prefer to call all people in an organisation who are responsible for others leaders or coaches. It tends to change people's mindset about their role.)

From a time-investment point of view, the pilot may have some more time freedom than the driver, but their time is still very much linked to the business. They can go away for a couple of weeks and things should run fine while they are gone, but any longer than that and some things may come to a standstill.

The pilot is still making all medium-to-major decisions. They may have some people in key positions running various departments (sales, marketing, finance, operations, etc) but are commonly still wearing many of these hats themselves. Each department of the business has a level of support, with the largest portion of the team usually employed in operations (getting the work out the door).

The problems at pilot level might look like this.

- Ownership mentality: hard to get others to think like you as an owner.
- Freedom: still tied heavily to the business – time freedom is limited
- People problems: an ever-growing share of the overall problems to be solved and source of stress simply due to numbers and the complexity of having more people.
- Cash: short of cash for growth. Cash flow can still be an issue.

When a pilot-level business is running well, here is what it can look like:

- strong levels of profitability and cash flow (well above industry averages)
- significant levels of time freedom for the owner (2- to 3-week holidays are very achievable at this stage)
- ease of hiring due to a strong, healthy culture and the team running the hiring process
- good access to financing due to a strong balance sheet and profitability
- solid business valuations due to less owner reliance (although not complete) and strong financials. Easier to sell.

THE OWNER

The owner is time-free from their business as much as they ever can be. The illusion that you can own a business and spend your days sitting on a beach sipping Mai Tais is a myth that sounds very attractive; however, as far as I've seen, has never been achieved successfully. Look at the larger private companies, and you will find an owner who is still engaged at some level (eg Michael Dell, Larry Page, Elon Musk, Richard Branson).

The exceptions to this might be family businesses where the outgoing generation has disengaged but still retains ownership. This is certainly an option if you are a family business, but I would suggest that fully disengaging is a dangerous prospect no matter how much you trust the next generation, particularly if your ownership also creates liability. Another exception is where the owner has an absolute rock star right-hand person who is in there running the business.

The reality is, even in these situations, most people at the owner level are still mentally and emotionally tied to the business. So while your physical time may be free, mentally and emotionally you are still invested.

The straightforward way to know if you are in the owner position is if you can be absent from your business for extended periods of time, yet the business continues to run well and continues to grow.

As the owner, while you are not necessarily physically present, you are still engaged and active in the business. You are coaching your leadership team, minding a pulse on the market (customers, competitors, trends etc) and have a strong say in the vision and direction of the company. This is not a hands-off role, which is a very important distinction to make. Of course, you are free to *choose* to be completely out; I just could not endorse that as a sustainable path.

A business is like any living thing – if you don't pay attention to it, nurture it and feed it, it will die. While you may have other people doing the feeding, it's rare that you can completely disengage.

Typical problems at the owner level might include the following.

- Identification issues: it can be hard to identify if problems are internal or external (due to the quality of information from your leadership team). For example, are sales low because of the market, or the skills of your sales and marketing teams?
- Reacting to changes in the market: a larger business takes more energy to move and change than a smaller one.
- Error costs: mistakes at this level can cost a lot more.

- Finding the right leadership team: high levels of trust are required here.

When things are working well at the owner level, it might look like this.
- You would have a full-time CEO or president as well as a leadership team that runs the business day-to-day.
- You will be involved in a meeting rhythm with your team and will have access to a real-time dashboard feeding you key information on the health of the business. This could be done remotely.
- There are strong levels of profitability and cash flow (well above industry averages).
- You have geographical freedom.
- The business has the ability to attract great people.
- You have good access to financing due to a strong balance sheet and profitability, and/or less reliance on outside financing.
- You have remarkable business valuations. The business is easy to sell as you may now be attractive to bigger institutional buyers.

While all this sounds great, it's rare that you are completely free. You still have obligations, as we've already pointed out. To become completely free, you will need to exit the business altogether, which is the subject of another book entirely.

The owner is in an enviable position. The roadmap to scale to this level (as with each level below) is the subject of this book. It's up to you to determine which stage is the right one for your business – and your life goals.

THE FOUR KEYS
FRAMEWORK

NOW WE GET into the meat of this book.

In this section, we cover our framework and methodology for growing your business to the level you want. We call the framework the Four Keys. It's the framework I use for my own businesses and the framework we use with our clients. The Four Keys are simple without being simplistic, which makes the otherwise complex topic of business growth more easily understood and actioned.

The Four Keys refer to the four major areas of every business that must be developed and mastered (at some level) for sustainability to be achieved. As a business owner, you need to have a level of competency over all four areas. As your business grows, you will delegate some, or all, of the areas; however, that does not absolve you of the responsibility to know your stuff before you do.

The Four Keys are:

1. money
2. growth
3. operations
4. people.

Figure 2 shows the Four Keys in context of a ship. The analogy is simple. A ship's purpose is to navigate from its starting point to its destination successfully. For it to do that, many things must be in place. A ship must have a skipper, it needs to be clear on its destination, it must have a planned route, and the people on board need to know how to control the ship and, most importantly, have the skills to get things back on course when they veer off.

To take the analogy further, I've used a cargo ship showing four cargo holds. These holds represent the Four Keys.

A warning here that there will be many strange and wonderful analogies ahead to solidify these concepts, so let's dive into it. Strap yourself in!

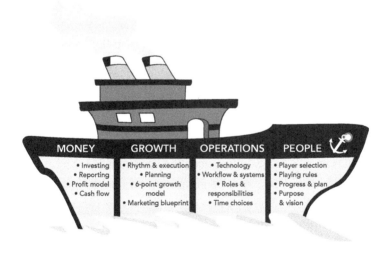

FIGURE 2: THE FOUR KEYS

MONEY

WE ALL WANT MORE of it, yet it's surprisingly common for business owners to be relatively uneducated when it comes to understanding money. I'm not talking about understanding what money is, but how it flows, how you measure it and how you manage it.

Yes, I'm talking about financials and cash-flow management. There is a direct correlation between your level of financial literacy and the financial health of your business, period. Wanting better financial results without having the right level of financial knowledge is like wanting to lose weight without knowing the basics of diet and exercise. To achieve results in any area, you first need the base knowledge.

(*Note*: if you are already groaning and feel the topic of financials bores you to tears, please know this is a surprisingly common trait among business owners, so you're not alone. Look at the end of this section to see the massive profit and cash gains that can be generated by knowing this stuff. Hopefully, that should give you the motivation to soldier through it.)

Before we dive into the nitty-gritty of the Money Key, let me take a moment to share a story about one of our clients, Paul. It illustrates how there can often be many problems in growing a business sustainably, but knowing the order in which to address things is critical.

In this section, I'll be referring to your financial statements in various ways. If at any stage you don't know what I'm talking about, watch my video 'Understanding your financial statements' in the resource section of the companion website (jumpingoffthewheel.com).

Case study: Paul's story

Paul is a home renovator specialising in exterior finishes. Think roofing, cladding, windows, gutters and so on. He is a brilliant tradesman, and you will struggle to find someone who can do better work than Paul. Subsequently, his business has grown largely through word of mouth due to the magnificent work he does. Paul has an additional competitive advantage in that he's a clean freak, which anyone who has hired a renovator will appreciate. When Paul has finished a job, not only will you be completely amazed by the quality of his artistry, but your home will probably be cleaner than when he started. This is rare for a tradesperson. And for Paul, it's enough to ensure a high level of repeat and referral work.

Now, at the outset this is great, proving industry knowledge and skills do pay off in growing your business. But, what you don't see is the level of chaos that was in Paul's life. Because Paul was busy, he needed to hire some help, but for some reason, he always seemed to hire the wrong person. This resulted in lots of wasted time from repeated training and excessive time spent recruiting and being let down by no-shows, not to mention the financial cost of all these time-wasting activities. The result was that much of the time Paul was less productive than he could be on his own. But he was trying to grow his business and increase his capacity. Paul felt he was letting his customers down when he couldn't do their work or service their referrals.

On top of the staff issues, Paul's finances were a mess. He always seemed to be short on cash and frequently found himself thinking, 'Where is all the money? I'm working long hours, but the money doesn't seem to be showing up as it should.'

To say Paul worked long hours is an understatement. Paul barely had a holiday because when he did take one, the money (which always seemed to be tight) stopped coming in almost completely, not to mention the work that piled up while he was away. This was primarily because his employees were less productive because they required supervision and guidance to be at their best.

The result was that the freedom and joy Paul dreamed of getting from his business seemed a long way off and he found it hard to see how to make it different. After all, he was exceptional at his work and people loved his work, and he never had to spend any money on marketing. Paul's dominant thought was, 'What the %*#$ am I doing wrong?' Paul was caught in the hamster wheel.

PAUL'S TURNAROUND

When we first met Paul and he shared his story with us, we heard many of the issues and challenges we'd heard many times before: 'Cash flow is tight', 'It's so hard to find good people', 'I'm starting to feel burnt out', 'It was much easier and more profitable when it was just me.' And Paul didn't seem to take much comfort when we told him he wasn't alone (nor should he). What Paul wanted to know was how to fix it.

Our starting point was to share with Paul the Four Keys framework and how it applies to building a successful driver-level business. Of course, Paul didn't know he was building a driver business, so when we shared this model with him, he could see that is exactly what he was after – a business that, while it did require him to run it consistently, would provide him with healthy cash flow and the ability to take decent vacations each year.

Paul was not looking to build the next multinational corporation. He simply wanted a small business that ran well – one that gave him financial stability, a healthy work–life balance and a feeling of satisfaction knowing he had created something that allowed him to achieve the first two outcomes. In my experience, this is what many small business owners are looking for.

Once Paul saw the model for a successful driver business, he could see several areas that were creating problems for him. The one that stood out for Paul was the people side. We affirmed his observation that if he could fix the people issues, that would free up a lot of time and relieve a lot of stress for him.

We then guided Paul to his financial numbers and asked the following question, 'What are the consequences to you and the business of your tight cash flow?' He thought for a while, and at first, it seemed like a mild state of depression overcame his facial expressions. In a weaker voice, he told us about the impact it was having at home. He explained how his wife was quite concerned about their future, as was he.

They didn't have any major investments aside from the business (which didn't hold a lot of value in its current state) and their home. He also said that the tight cash flow meant he was always feeling a bit stressed when mistakes happened or if a new hire took longer to train than he wanted. And if a customer took a particularly long time to pay, it was a real squeeze.

Having brought these issues to the surface, we asked Paul what the impact would be on him and his business if these cash flow and profitability issues disappeared. What would it be like if he didn't have to worry about meeting his financial obligations week to week? If there were a healthy buffer that meant all would still be okay if he had a lean week or two?'

You can probably guess the response. While it seems like a no-brainer from an outsider's perspective, it's surprisingly common how often a client wants to start fixing an area that is important and necessary but is not the area that will have the greatest impact on their business. Paul wanted to start on the people problems. In his case (as in many others), that was not the right place to start. Nine times out of ten, fixing the money problems is always the place to start.

Lesson: unless you've got healthy cash reserves, working on strong cash flow and healthy profitability is always the number 1 priority.

Seeing the cloud of depression lift after answering this question, we asked Paul if we could slide in cash flow and profitability as the first priority.

There can be many problems or areas you feel you need to address, and no doubt, they are all important. It's critical that we identify the lead-domino problem or opportunity that will make all the others easier to fix.

In Paul's case, fixing the profitability or cash flow issue – at this early stage we were not sure exactly where the problem was, we just knew we needed a better flow of money coming in – would give him breathing space. And we knew it could be fixed because he had plenty of work, but he wasn't doing a decent job of converting plenty of work to plenty of money in the bank.

Lack of money in the bank can be a symptom of poor profitability or poor cash flow management. We would normally ask a few questions to see where the core problem lies, but in Paul's case, there were problems in both areas. We decided to start with cash flow, as changes can be made there to get instant results. Then, we shifted our focus to improve profitability which, when combined with the work on his cash flow, had a compounding effect when it came to money in the bank. And that made everyone happy. Once we had some quick wins on the money side, then we shifted focus to the people issues.

The Money segment of the Four Keys has four components.

1. Cash flow
2. Profit model
3. Data and reporting
4. Investing – capital allocation.

So, let's look at the first step – getting a handle on cash flow.

MAXIMISING AND MANAGING CASH FLOW: THE SLEEP-AT-NIGHT FACTOR

Healthy cash flow is a combination of doing a good job on profitability and converting those profits into cash. If your profitability is weak or negative, you can apply Band-Aid solutions for a while, but sooner or later the Band-Aid is going to fall off.

The reason we begin with cash flow is that cash is the reality. Cash is also what generally causes the problems (including stress). Once you can see the full picture of your cash flow, you can then make proactive changes, and often get immediate results – even if those results are just peace of mind!

My goal here is to give you basics that are enough to understand the critical element of your cash flow, but you may want to learn more than we'll cover here. The purpose of this book is to educate you on what you need to know and give you enough tools to get on your way and start seeing results. This topic really deserves a book in itself – there are plenty of good ones that have already been written.

A quick aside before we dive into cash flow management: I need to clarify the difference between profitability and cash flow. It's a distinction that often causes confusion and, if not understood, can have you running in circles.

Profitability versus cash flow – an enormous difference

The simplest explanation is that profit is a theory (a good theory nonetheless, but still a theory) and cash is reality. What that means is when you issue an invoice, it shows in your accounts as a sale (unless you are using the cash accounting method), but you don't see that money in your bank account until sometime later (hopefully within days) when you get paid. An invoice is a promise to be paid. Likewise, when you receive a bill, what you really have is a request to pay. When you get the bill and enter it into your accounting software, it shows as an expense immediately, but the money has not left your account yet, though it will sometime in the future, when you pay the bill.

So, when you look at your profit and loss, what you are really looking at is a list of promises for payment (sales) and requests for payment (bills). The profit at the bottom is what will happen if all these promises are kept.

So, it's all theory. And yes, it should be a good theory (again, hopefully), but in a lot of cases it does not relate very well to what you see in your bank account.

This is where business owners can get stuck because it is what is in the bank account that allows you to pay your bills and yourself. Conversely, that same bank balance is also what causes considerable stress, so having a feeling of control over it is a good thing. Let's look at that.

Managing cash flow is about two things:

1. forecasting: being able to predict cash needs and your cash position into the future
2. tweaking: knowing the levers to pull to make your cash flow as strong as possible.

Forecasting cash flow

How far you choose to predict your cash flow will depend on your needs. There will be times, like when you are seeking to finance, that you may need to prepare a longer-term forecast (eg 12 to 24 months), but for the everyday operation of your business, a 3- to 6-month forecast is usually sufficient. There will be exceptions, but if you're looking for a starting point, that is a good one.

If you'd like access to this tool, log on to our resource section and knock yourself out. There are full instructions within the tool to guide you.
jumpingoffthewheel.com

With our clients, we use a tool called the sleep-at-night tool. Essentially, this is a template that provides you with the ability to forecast incoming and outgoing cash in a way that breaks down your cash position on a weekly or monthly basis.

Figure 3 shows what it looks like.

salesup! FUELLING YOUR GROWTH	Cashflow Forecasting			
	Week1	Week2	Week3	Week4
OPERATING ACC.	1-Jan-18	8-Jan-18	15-Jan-18	22-Jan-18
CASH IN				
Sales (Operations)	$ 21,000.00	$10,200.00	$9,900.00	$13,400.00
Sale of Assets (Investing)				
Borrowing (Financing)				
(A) Total Cash In	**$ 21,000.00**	**$10,200.00**	**$9,900.00**	**$13,400.00**
OPERATING CASH OUT				
Inventory				
Supplier A	$2,000.00		$2,000.00	
Supplier B		$500.00		$500.00
Supplier C		$3,000.00		$3,000.00
Operating Expenses				
Rent		$1,500.00		
Utilities				
Payroll	$8,000.00		$8,000.00	
VISA				$3,500.00
GST		$12,000.00		
Payroll Liabilities				
Advisors		$3,000.00		
Purchase of Assets (Investing)				
Repay Borrowings (Financing)				
SH withdrawal				
(B) Total Cash Out	**$8,000.00**	**$16,500.00**	**$8,000.00**	**$3,500.00**
(A-B) Surplus or Deficit	**$13,000.00**	**$(6,300.00)**	**$1,900.00**	**$9,900.00**
Beginning Cash	$5,000.00	$18,000.00	$11,700.00	$13,600.00
Ending Cash	$18,000.00	$11,700.00	$13,600.00	$23,500.00

FIGURE 3: CASH FLOW FORECAST

Tweaking your cash flow: knowing which levers to pull

Now that you have a handle on what your cash flow looks like today and into the future, we can switch gears into a more proactive mode and look at how you can improve it.

To make sense of the numbers we are about to discuss, you might find it helpful to print off a cash statement or statement of cash flows report from your accounting software to refer to as we go along. This report is different from your profit and loss (P&L) statement in that it just shows actual movements of cash. Your P&L, as already discussed, is a summary of the promises for payment that have been made – it's the theory portion. For this exercise, we're dealing with fact.

There are three core sections that make up your overall cash flow (shown on your cash statement). They are operating cash flow, investing cash flow and financing cash flow. These are accounting terms, so let's explain them.

(*Note*: remember, we are talking about cash flow, not profitability. Some of the items below will be related to profitability and will show up on your P&L statement, and some will not.)

Operating cash flow (OCF) refers to transactions that relate to everyday business operations (ie buying stock, collecting money from customers, paying staff, bills, etc). Many of these transactions will also be on your P&L. When they show up on your P&L, that is the promise part. When they show up on your cash statement, that is the reality part. It's when the money actually changes hands.

Investing cash flow (ICF) refers to transactions involving purchase or sale of equipment. For example, if you buy a car, building or piece of equipment, it won't show up on your P&L, but money will come out of your bank account – this is investing cash flow.

Financing cash flow (FCF) refers to any transaction involving the borrowing or repaying of loans. It also involves money that is invested in the company (by you, the owners or by outside investors) or distributed from the company in the form of dividends. Again, these transactions will not show up on your P&L, but will cause your bank balance to go up and down.

All three of these categories are important and affect your cash flow. That said, the one we really want to be on top of (and the one that needs to be super healthy) is the OCF.

Think of your OCF as the heart pumping the blood through your business. FCF is like receiving a blood transfusion (money in) or donating blood (money out), and ICF is like (warning – this is analogy is about to get even weirder) adding or subtracting a limb that requires blood to pump through it. (I warned you.)

If the heart is weak at pumping (poor OCF), the body (your business) will be weak, and you won't have the ability to buy extra limbs (invest in assets to help you grow) because you have not got the blood to support them. And you will need to get transfusions (borrow money) to stay alive. Infusions of cash will only last so long because sooner or later people won't want to keep giving you blood because they can see you're dying (ie there is no hope of that blood being returned and their loans aren't going to be repaid).

However, when you have a strong heart pumping lots of blood (strong OCF), you don't need infusions (to borrow money), and you have a surplus of blood to either purchase extra limbs (hire people, buy assets that will help make sales) or donate blood for uses outside your body (dividends or investments).

Okay, enough of the weird analogy. Hopefully, you get the point. OCF is the lifeblood of your business, and it's the one we need to watch the closest. It's the one that determines whether our business is healthy or weak. So, let's look at what drives it.

Operating cash flow (OCF)

Operating cash flow (OCF), as we've said, involves all movements of cash relating to everyday business operations; namely, the buying and selling of stuff and the paying of bills associated with running the business. There are three main drivers of OCF. They are:

1. receivables (money owed to you by your customers)
2. payables (money you owe to suppliers)
3. inventory (stock you are holding ready for sale; for some businesses, this won't be applicable).

As we've already discussed, when we make a sale, we don't always get the money at that moment. When we don't, that transaction becomes a receivable (money you are due to receive). That is the first driver of operating cash flow – how long it takes you to collect that money. Some terms you'll hear that refer to this are *receivable days*, *collection days* or *day's sales outstanding* (DSOs).

✓ When you collect your receivables faster, this is good for OCF.

✗ When you collect your receivables slower, this is bad for OCF.

On the flip side, when you receive a bill that you need to pay but you don't pay right away (because you have terms with your vendor), that transaction becomes a payable (a bill you need to pay). So, our second driver of OCF is *payable days*.

✓ When you pay your payables slower, this is good for OCF.

✗ When you pay your payables faster, this is bad for OCF.

Obviously, there is a balance point here. If you take too long to pay people, you may damage relationships and may be cut off from suppliers. That said, it's possible to negotiate longer terms, but we'll get to that.

Now, if you are a business that holds inventory, this is your third driver of OCF. If you don't have inventory, you're off the hook for this one. In short, the less inventory you hold on the shelves, and the faster you sell what you do have, the better for OCF. We call this measure *inventory days* or *inventory turns*. It's basically the measure of how long inventory sits on your shelves before being sold.

✓ When your inventory sells faster, this is good for OCF.

✗ When your inventory sells slower, this is bad for OCF.

Think of inventory on the shelves as bundles of cash. The more that is on the shelves, and the longer it stays there, the less of that money is in your bank account and the less that money is making money. Now let's look at how you use these three cash flow drivers in practice.

The first step is to measure each of the drivers (receivable days, payable days and inventory days). Once we can see how each are currently sitting, we can play around with some what-ifs and take a look at where the opportunities lie in your business.

1. To calculate receivable days, use the following formula.

(average receivables/sales) x number of days in period

Where:
- average receivables = (starting receivables + ending receivables)/2.

(*Note*: you'll get starting and ending receivables from the two balance sheets that bookend the period you are measuring; that is, if you wanted to measure receivable days for the first calendar quarter, January–March, you'll need the balance sheet for 31 December of the previous year (this will be your starting balance sheet) and 31 March of the current year (this will be your ending balance sheet). Take the receivables numbers from both those balance sheets, add them together and then divide by 2.

Let's work with an example to give us some better context. John's Widgets has annual sales of $1,000,000, and on average, its receivables are $125,000. We would calculate its receivable days as follows.

($125,000/$1,000,000) x 365 = 45.63 days

This means that on average, it takes John's Widgets 45.63 days to collect from its customers.

2. To calculate payable days, use the following formula:

(average payables/[COGS + expenses]) x number of days in period

Where:
- average payables = (starting payable + ending payable)/2
- COGS = cost of goods sold or direct costs
- expenses = fixed costs (basically all other costs not included in COGS aside from non-cash expenses – see below).

(To learn more, see jumpingoffthewheel.com.)

Just like the average receivables, you'll get the average

payables from the same balance sheets.

COGS + expenses is basically every operating cost you incurred during the period. These will be found on your P&L statement. (Do not include non-cash expenses in this calculation. Non-cash expenses are things that appear on your P&L, but you don't have to pay for. Depreciation and amortisation are the two most common examples.)

For John's Widgets, the numbers are as follows:
- time period: 90 days (one quarter)
- average payables = $50,000
- COGS + expenses = $225,000

Therefore, the payable days are:
- ($50,000/$225,000) x 90 = 20 days

This means that, on average, it takes John's Widgets 20 days to pay its bills.

3. To calculate inventory days, use the following formula.

(average inventory value/COGS) x days in period

For John's Widgets, the inventory numbers are:
- average inventory value = $100,000 (Just like the average receivable and payable days, you'll work this one out the same way using a beginning and ending balance sheet.)
- COGS = $150,000 (Taken straight from the P&L statement, be sure you only include materials and not direct labour when calculating your own.)
- Inventory days = ($100,000/$150,000) x 90 = 60 days.

75

This means that, on average, a piece of inventory sits on the shelf for 60 days before it's sold.

In summary, the operating cash flow drivers for John's Widgets are:

- receivable days – 46
- payable days – 20
- inventory days – 60

Now, let's see how we can improve this.

Starting with receivable days, we would overhaul the accounts receivable (AR) process (assuming there was one to start with). This includes how you set and communicate your terms with clients, and how you follow up and enforce those terms.

Here are some tips to keep in mind when designing your AR system.

1. Your terms: don't assume you need to give the same terms that everyone else in your industry is giving. You can put yourself in a strong position to institute much shorter terms (even getting full payment in advance) when you have a strong reputation and people want to work with you.

2. Ask for deposits: if you can't get full payment up front, position a deposit. I've even seen it work in industries that never ask for deposits; rather than requiring clients to pay a deposit, when someone booked a job we simply asked, 'Would you like to leave a deposit to ensure your schedule is met?' About half the people gave a 50 per cent deposit. Great!

3. Make it easier to pay: accept credit cards and all forms of payment you possibly can, including online payment options.

4. Clearly communicate your terms: this means in your verbal and written communications, (quotes, invoices, emails and so on).

5. Proactive calls: put in a call a few days before payment is due to ask if the client has everything they need to process payment on time. For example: 'We just wanted to make sure you had all the information you needed to process our invoice on the due date.' The more your client sees that you are on top of your AR, the more likely your bill will be at the top of the list.

6. Get the accounts payable (AP) person onside: when you get to know who pays the bills, having them on your side goes a long way. When they are looking at which bills to pay out of their (possibly limited) bank account, often the ones that get paid are for businesses they like or need. Be both.

7. Recognise clients: in follow-up to the point above, consider a note or a small gift to the person who processes your invoices to celebrate their continued on-time payments. It's not a bribe, but it does let them know how much you appreciate their business and it makes for smoother payment processing.

8. Past-due payment calls: when clients miss the due date, be on it. The best approach is to be polite and respectful yet also assertive (think First Principle The Respect Matrix). And be consistent in your follow-up. There is no need to be unpleasant or aggressive, at this stage at least! Take notes on what was said and agreed to, then follow up when you say you will or when they say they will do something but don't.

9. Cut off supply: have strict terms on when you will cut off

service to a client for non-payment – and stick to it.

10. Go to collections: on the rare occasion that people really string you out, have a collections service you can outsource to. I've also seen it work well to send a demand letter from a lawyer.

Back to John's Widgets. What if, through some better receivables management, it could get its receivable days from the current 46 down to 35? What would that look like for cash flow? Let's take a look. To work it out we just reverse-engineer the formula.

> **(target receivable days/days in period) x sales = new average receivables**

So, (35/365) x $1,000,000 = $95,890 (with rounding).

The starting receivable days were $125,000, so that would mean roughly an extra **$29,000** in the bank ($125,000 – $95,890). Not a bad result for some strategies that cost the company nothing.

Moving our attention to payable days, John's Widgets is paying its bills, on average, 20 days after getting them. This is pretty quick. I'm sure its suppliers love this, but I think it is paying faster than it needs to. Let's say that on review, we decided that 28 days was a good target. It would still keep the company in the good books with suppliers, but would allow it to get better use of its cash by keeping it in its bank account a little longer.

Again, when we reverse-engineer the formula, this is how it would play out.

(new payable days/days in period) x (COGS + expenses) = new average payables

So, (28/90) x $225,000 = $70,000.

So, this means if it now pays its bills in 28 days on average instead of 20 days, it would have an extra **$20,000** in its bank account. Again, not bad for a strategy that costs nothing.

Lastly, let's look at inventory days. The current status is 60 days, which is giving the company an inventory value of $100,000. Here are some tips for reducing inventory days.

1. Measure it.
2. Make someone accountable for the target number of inventory days.
3. Find the slow-moving stock and blow it out. This is often worth doing even if you lose money on it. With the freed-up cash, you can reinvest in stock that moves.
4. Implement or refine your reorder levels.
5. Find suppliers who can deliver faster and/or more frequently, which means you don't need to carry as much stock (known as a just-in-time shipping strategy, or JIT).
6. Merchandising. In store (if you have one), on your website or in your sales people's sales kit. Know what you want to sell more of and put a focus on it.
7. Incentivise your sales team – in the car sales world, they call it spiffs. The incentives change regularly as the needs of inventory movement change.
8. Carry fewer stock-keeping units. Make use of the 80/20 principle and boil your selection down to the items that are really moving. You might not go right down to your

top 20 per cent, but you could almost certainly get rid of your bottom 20 per cent.

Now, if through using some of these strategies to manage its inventory better, John's Widgets could get inventory days down to 45, what would that mean to the company? Again, we reverse-engineer the formula, like this:

> **(target number of inventory days/days in period) x COGS = new inventory level**

So, (45/90) x $150,000 = $75,000

The inventory, at 60 days, was $100,000. Reducing inventory days down to 45 makes inventory $75,000, meaning an extra **$25,000** sitting in the bank account instead of out there on the shelves.

When we consolidate the positive changes to all three operating cash flow drivers for John's Widgets, here's where we end up.

- AR days – extra $29,000 cash
- AP days – extra $20,000 cash
- inventory days – extra $25,000 cash
- total boost in OCF – $74,000.

For a business that is doing $1,000,000 in total sales, I would consider $74,000 of extra cash a pretty decent result, wouldn't you?

Case study: Beth's cash flow

Beth had been in business for around 17 years and had overcome her fair share of challenges (the latest being cancer). Her business challenges were focused on cash flow and growth, and she reluctantly chose to engage us. (She confided later that her initial thoughts were, 'What can these bozos teach me about my business?')

The interesting thing when we started working with Beth was that she had considerable knowledge about cash flow, but was simply overwhelmed with the day-to-day operations and had lost sight of some of the basics.

The first thing we did was measure her receivable days, which came out at 53 days. Beth's business was doing around $2,000,000 in sales, which meant that at any one time its receivables were around $290,410 ([2,000,000/365] x 53).

We asked Beth what she believed a realistic receivables goal would be over the next 90 days and she came up with 45 days.

From there, we looked at how receivables were currently being managed. In short, they weren't. Without wasting time, we engaged the person responsible for collections and had a brainstorming session on best practices.

We showed them our collections system, and from there we implemented and tweaked different areas. We also asked the employee in charge of collections what they believed was a realistic goal over the next 90 days, and they came back with 40 days. So, we settled on the 45-day goal that everyone could buy into. We implemented daily tracking which, when combined with the new systems, really put the focus on their goal.

The end results? After 90 days the business had achieved a receivables average of 44 days. That meant an extra $50,000 in its bank account. But we didn't stop there. For the next successive 90-day periods we continued to set goals, and continued with this format until the business was hovering consistently around the 32-day mark (down from 53) and $115,000 in positive cash flow. Not too shabby.

After we'd addressed Beth's AR, we turned our attention to her inventory. Beth's business was a mix of plastics distribution and light manufacturing, and both those elements required inventory.

Just like with AR, Beth knew about inventory days, but it had not been in focus due to other day-to-day hamster wheel issues.

The first step, of course, was to measure the current inventory days score. When we did this, we came out with a measurement of 91 inventory days. In case you don't have to deal with inventory and don't have a feel for it, for this business that number was high.

Now that we knew there was some opportunity here, we took the following steps:

1. looked at what was moving and what was not
2. reviewed existing inventory and re-ordering practices.

As discussed in First Principles, the 80:20 rule certainly applies here. In most cases, roughly 20 per cent of inventory is doing 80 per cent of the selling. If we look at this in reverse, 20 per cent is probably not moving at all. We wanted to look to see if this was true in Beth's case.

And it almost was. We found just over 10 per cent that

was not moving at all. From the $334,000 worth of total inventory, $40,000 worth had been there for over a year. So, we decided to discount it heavily to move it out the door and ended up getting $30,000 for it. Remember, dead inventory (ie inventory that is not selling) is like cash sitting on the shelf that you can't use. We needed to make it useable.

Yes, we took a $10,000 loss on those sales, but we freed up $30,000 in cash that was sitting on the shelves. That cash we used to help pay down the line of credit. We also could have (if the business needed it, which in this case, it didn't) reinvested that money in inventory that was moving and making money.

The next step was to look at the systems the business was using to manage the inventory. In short, it was pretty much a free-for-all. If someone thought they needed to order something, they did. That provides lots of freedom for the team, but produces a disaster for inventory.

In summary, cash flow can be one of those things that just happens and does not get a whole lot of attention. Like most things, the level of attention you give something, the more it will perform for you. Take this knowledge, whether it is new to you or a refresher, and look for the areas to optimise your cash flow. Your stress hormones will thank you for it!

YOUR PROFIT MODEL

The second component of the Money section is your *profit model*.

Everyone gets excited when we talk about growing a business. But when we only go after top-line growth and making sales, we often do it at the expense of maximising profits.

Remember, to grow a business in a sustainable and smart manner, you need cash. And to generate cash, you almost always need profit. So, no matter the growth goal, always keep profitability in your focus.

In this section, I'm going to introduce you to the simple profit model that underpins every business on the planet. It's not complicated, and it's not sexy, but it's vital to the health of your business.

Basically, once you make a sale, that money needs to cover five distinct areas relating to profitability:

1. cost of materials – that is assuming you have materials (eg retail and manufacturing)
2. cost of direct labour – the labour that produces what you sell
3. cost of indirect labour – the labour you need to run the business regardless of how much you sell (eg management and admin)
4. overhead costs – otherwise known as fixed costs or expenses (eg rent, phones, utilities etc)
5. profit – what's left over after you've covered off the other four.

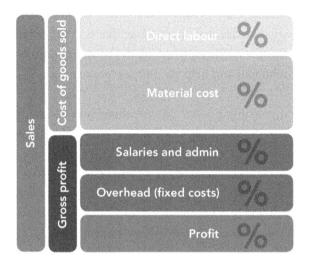

FIGURE 4: PROFIT MODEL

The key to knowing your profit model is knowing what percentage should be allocated to each area. Put graphically, it looks like Figure 4 above.

While this graphic looks simple, it may not be as simple and straightforward in practice. Here are the steps to work out your percentages.

- Step 1: Have clean historical numbers you can use for reference. I recommend at least six months' worth. Ideally, you would always have clean numbers, but I know some of us are better than others at keeping our numbers up to date and accurate.
- Step 2: Look back historically at what your percentages have been. Compare periods where you can to understand variations and anomalies. You are looking to build a model that best represents your business on average.

- Step 3: Do you like what you see? In other words, do you like the profit percentage that is at the bottom? If the answer is yes, great job. If it's no, then we need to rebuild it and help you to make some tough decisions.

Your starting point when tweaking your model is with your COGS. You really need to have a workable gross margin (gross profit/sales) that allows for a profitable business. If your gross margin is 20 per cent, and sales are $300,000, it's going to be hard to run a profitable business. You will only have $60,000 to cover overhead and have profit leftover.

The gross profit margin you should be aiming for will depend on your business. (*Note*: if you're not sure what it should be, search for your industry average, then add a few points. The average is never a good target because most businesses in your industry are not doing very well.)

Once you've got your gross margin set where you think it should be, decide on your level of profitability. Again, work in percentages. To give you an idea, 10 per cent for most businesses is somewhat acceptable. More than 15% per cent is starting to look nice and healthy, and once you're in the 20 per cents, you're talking a strong business.

Keep in mind that these examples are all generalisations. If you are a start-up or micro business (<$500,000 sales), aiming for 20 per cent net profit is most likely going to be hard. Again, there are always exceptions (service-based businesses being a common one). The end goal comes down to knowing what type of business you're in and having a model that works.

(*Note*: in these calculations, be sure to include your salary somewhere. Don't delude yourself into thinking you are profitable by not paying yourself. True profitability is after owner's compensation (unless you do not work in the business). And your compensation should reflect fair market rates. In other words, if you had to hire someone to do what you do, how much would you have to pay them?)

Once you've established your desired profit percentage for your current business size, you can now work out your overhead, salaries and admin percentage that is left over.

For example, if you decide that your gross margin should be 40 per cent and you want 10 per cent net profit, you're left with 30 per cent to spend on overhead and salaries. If you're a $1,000,000 business, that gives you $300,000 to spend.

You now need to create an operating budget for overhead that is less than $300,000. Chances are you are going to be faced with some hard spending decisions, which is the whole point.

In making your decision on where to expend money, use this concept to guide you – there are only two reasons to spend money in business.

1. To keep customers
2. To get more customers.

Anything outside of this is pimping your ride. And you will be amazed to discover when forced to make the hard spending decisions where you may be pimping your ride.

Using this customer-focused lens helps highlight where the pimping may be happening.

Effects of growth on profitability

So, what happens if you want to grow, but your $300,000 overhead budget, which needs to include salaries and admin wages, doesn't allow enough for the marketing you will need to make that growth happen? You'll need to review your profit target.

When you are in growth mode, investment will be required, and profitability may suffer, and it's okay to make that decision if you know your end game will net a return on that marketing investment.

Choose to invest in effective marketing to create growth that will add value to your company. Doing the exercise above will ensure you are making informed and intentional decisions rather than shooting from the hip and hoping it will all work out.

Another crucial point is understanding your tiers of fixed-cost investment. As you grow, you will likely incur additional overhead costs. This may come from staff you need to hire, larger facilities you need to rent or similar costs. At the point you choose to invest in these costs, your economies of scale and percentage of overhead will be out of whack. It may look something like Figure 5.

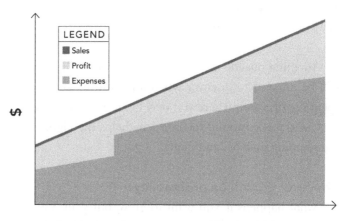

FIGURE 5: PROFITABILITY THROUGH GROWTH

The representation in Figure 5 is fine in theory, as long as you keep growing and your gross margin holds to target. Eventually, you will grow into the capacity you have created. And most probably, once you do grow into the additional capacity, your overhead percentage will be lower than it was before you made the investment in additional overhead.

When you compare the economies of scale or overhead percentage of well-run larger companies, they are almost always more efficient than their smaller counterparts. There are tiers of efficiency as you grow, which means you'll have varying levels of achievable profitability as your company grows.

DATA AND REPORTING

The third component of the Money Key is data and reporting. As Peter Drucker, commonly known as the father of management thinking famously said, 'What gets measured gets managed.'

Working out your cash flow and profit model is good, but if you never look at them again, they won't stay strong. Having meaningful, timely and accurate reporting is critical to keeping your numbers in line and feeling the pulse of your business. The starting point is to be looking at your income statement and balance sheet. The critical financial statement that most people ignore is the cash statement.

We need to look at all three financial statements and look for trends over time. Looking at any one in isolation or without comparison against various time periods often tells us very little, or worse, makes things look better than they are.

Looking at all three statements tells the complete story, so you'll want to know how to read and interpret them.

If the thought of interpreting these reports causes your left eye to start twitching, check out the videos in our resource section for a pain-free explanation.
jumpingoffthewheel.com

While these statements are useful, and you should be looking at them at least monthly, I think it's even better to design your own report that just shows the key numbers that really drive your business. We call this your financial dashboard.

Some of the numbers on your dashboard will come from the three key financial reports (P&L, balance sheet, cash statement); for example, total sales will be calculations from those reports (eg gross profit margins, receivable days, labour efficiency ratio (LER)) and other measurements that will be meaningful to your business (eg rework rates, quote conversion rate, gross profit dollars per day).

Your goal is to get a one-page report that can tell you exactly what is going on in your business at a high level. It won't give you all the details, but it will tell you what areas might require a closer look. For instance, if you look at your dashboard and the number that stands out is inventory days, you can then explore that further. Perhaps a large order was just received or perhaps reorder levels have not been adjusted properly for changes in the market. Whatever it is, you'll know to investigate further because the measurement is out of the parameters you have set for it.

Developing a dashboard is not usually done overnight. It's something that will evolve as your level of financial sophistication goes up, as you develop better ways of tracking and have more reliable numbers.

It's pointless to develop a dashboard if it takes someone 10 hours each week to compile the information. That is more than likely not a good use of time. The information should already exist in your systems somewhere. If there is something you want to measure but don't have the information handy, you can highlight that as something to develop in the future.

An effective dashboard is a living tool, and with technology and cloud computing today, it's possible to have live dashboards with real-time data that you can view on your smartphone from anywhere in the world, allowing you to step off the hamster wheel and keep tabs on the critical measures during your downtime. Pretty cool if you ask me.

Figure 6 is a sample dashboard we developed with one of our clients, a physiotherapy practice. Some of the key drivers of the business are unique to a healthcare service (eg client treatment completion rates, referral rates for doctors and patients, and appointment no-shows to name a few). Tracking these numbers helped our client stay on top of potential problems and head them off before they became massive issues.

To get started on your dashboard, start simple, using perhaps five to seven metrics from the following list. Make sure they are easy to compile, then start using them in your weekly meetings (see the Rhythm and execution section).

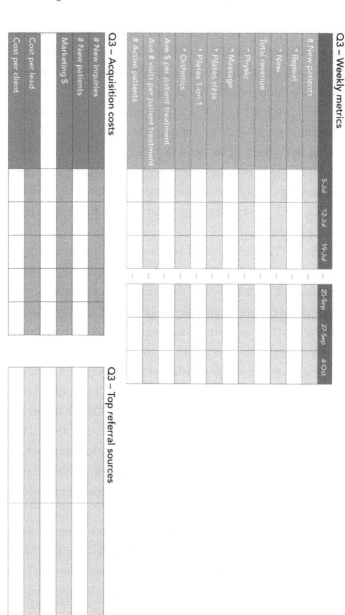

FIGURE 6: SAMPLE DASHBOARD

- sales
- sales compared to same time last year/month/quarter or versus budget
- receivables
- receivable days
- payables
- payable days
- inventory turns
- top 5 (or pick a number) customers by sales
- overtime
- waste and rework
- discounts
- number of web-site-unique visitors
- lead conversion rates (see Growth section)
- enquiries from website
- average order size
- wages/sales
- wages/profit
- billable time
- gross profit $/hr
- work in progress (WIP)
- number of demonstrations
- percentage of sales that are new business

INVESTING – CAPITAL ALLOCATION

The fourth and last component of the Money Key of our Four Keys framework is known as investing – capital allocation. Essentially, this means choosing how to handle the money needs of your business. This can involve money that is borrowed or invested in the business, or can relate to what to do with excess cash in the business.

Your business will always need working capital. In simple terms, that means the money you need to keep operations going. It's your buffer that will make your cash flow work and it bridges the gap between payables and receivables.

In addition to working capital, you may need money for capital expenditures such as real estate or equipment. Or, you may be embarking on a massive growth initiative that requires unusual amounts of cash to fund.

In short, capital allocation is about always making sure you have the cash you need and/or managing excess cash in the business.

We've covered a bit of this in our section on cash flow. The other major components of investing are:

- how to finance growth (from profits or outside funding)
- how much profits should be retained (linked to point above)
- what to do with excess cash (distribute/invest/debt reduction)
- what investments make sense and the best way to structure them.

This is some fun stuff to get into, and it's a critical component to understand when you are at that point in your business.

Realistically, this is a large topic and well beyond the scope of this book. If this is an area you want to learn more about, I'd suggest grabbing a copy of my recommended reading list from the download section of our companion site (jumpingoffthewheel.com). There are several books there that do an excellent job covering this topic.

For additional resources on Capital Allocation, check out my recommended reading list in the 'Resource' section on the website.
jumpingoffthewheel.com

GROWTH

GROWING YOUR COMPANY is what many consider to be the fun part of owning a business. It involves marketing and sales, and growing revenue. It's the glitz and glamour of the thing, and I would wholeheartedly agree with this statement. Sales and marketing involves a level of creativity and gives a good dose of dopamine when it all comes together. So, in some respects, sales and marketing can be like a drug.

I've already covered off the warnings of being purely top-line focused at the expense of bottom-line profitability, so there's no need to repeat it here. This can be a real threat to those of us who might tend to be sales and marketing addicts!

Okay, enough with the stern warnings, let's have some fun.

Before we jump into spending money on Google Ads, building an awesome website or creating social media accounts – in fact, before we invest any time or money in marketing – we need to answer a few fundamental questions that will guide us on how we'll make those marketing activities pay and be profitable.

Too often, business owners with the need to make sales just start doing everything they can think of relating to sales and marketing. They start throwing stuff out there in the hope that something sticks and works. I won't deny that when you start marketing, there is an element of seeing what works and what doesn't, but trying stuff out based on sound principles and assumptions is different from simply trying stuff out. The stories of businesses that invest disproportionate amounts of money into marketing with little return are all too common, and it doesn't have to be this way.

So, don't make that mistake, or if you have already, let's make sure you don't repeat it. From now on, all your marketing needs to be targeted, intentional and based on a blueprint that will give you the greatest chance of being profitable.

Note that I said, 'the greatest chance'. If there were a secret that made all marketing successful, that would be fantastic. But it doesn't exist. There are, however, fundamental principles that, when followed, greatly increase your chance of success. And only through consistent testing and measuring will you be able to find what works and what doesn't.

Because nothing is definite when deploying a marketing strategy, we always want to test it in some way that will guide us (without huge expense) on the likelihood of success. Sometimes testing is not feasible, but you want to use it whenever possible. The other side of this principle is measuring. There isn't much point testing without measuring. Where possible, we want to measure the results of our marketing efforts so that we have a pulse and some knowledge of what is working and what is not. Most marketing strategies are an educated guess about what is going to work. The only way to know for sure is to get the market to tell you.

Case study: Jason's lesson on testing

Jason and his wife Jacky had been running their used car dealership in Ontario, Canada, for around 20 years. They had done okay financially without really pushing the business, but now their eldest son had joined the business and they wanted to grow it. Jason and Jacky had managed very moderate growth levels by advertising regularly and servicing customers well, which resulted in repeat business. But when it came to accelerating that growth, they were a bit lost.

After looking at the numbers, it was clear an opportunity existed in lead generation. They were mainly advertising online and in print, which was the go-to medium for used cars at the time, and they were spending about $5,000 a month to do so.

We first implemented a simple measuring strategy of asking customers and potential customers where they heard about the dealership. After four weeks of collecting the information, they were stunned. While Autotrader (their chosen ad source) did bring in a considerable number of leads, only about 10 per cent came from the print version, with the remaining 90 per cent coming from online (this was back in 2006). Unsurprisingly, their bill with Autotrader was 80 per cent print and 20 per cent online.

It was clear we needed to change that. We also learned

that over 25 per cent of their leads were coming from referrals and they were doing nothing to thank those who referred them – a definite lost opportunity. These two opportunities came from the simple strategy of just asking people how they found out about them. The take-home lesson? If you do not measure your marketing, you are not in touch with what is working for you.

The Growth Key in the Four Keys comprises four sections:
1. your marketing blueprint
2. the 6-point growth model
3. planning
4. data and rhythm.
   Let's dive in.

YOUR MARKETING BLUEPRINT

The core of every company's marketing effort needs to stem from what we refer to as your marketing blueprint. The goal of your marketing blueprint is to identify your market niche; that is, where you can play in the market that will move you away from price competition so you know who your ideal customers are and *why* they are going to buy from *you*. To work this out, we need to explore the following areas.

- Your ideal customer. Who is your ideal customer? What are their traits and characteristics? What do they value and believe in?

- The problem. What is the problem that you solve for them? How would your customers describe this in their own language?
- Your core competency. What are you best at? What do you make good money doing? What do you enjoy doing the most? What can you scale most easily?
- Your competition. What are they good at and what makes them different? What are their strengths and core competencies? Why do people buy from them?
- Your unique selling proposition (USP). What makes you different? This comes from taking all four pieces above and refining the data into a clear and compelling value proposition or USP.

Knowing the answers to each of these questions allows you to determine what makes you different. Ideally, you need to be able to communicate this clearly and meaningfully to your ideal customer. This can be a complex task and one that might involve a substantial amount of thinking and refining.

That said, you don't need to have this perfected before you go out and start marketing. But you do need to have some clarity on the five areas of your marketing blueprint, which will allow your marketing efforts to be somewhat guided. Let's take a closer look at each of these five areas.

One more important note: these areas won't necessarily be addressed sequentially. In fact, how you respond to one area may influence another, and may require you to go back and review and refine. That is okay and is the intended flow of the process.

Your ideal customer

Knowing who to target is one of the most crucial parts of your marketing efforts. Many people get lost in trying to grow their business by serving everyone and anyone. The problem with that is, there will always be some people who don't resonate with what you are offering or the way you are offering it. It's best to focus your marketing toward those you know will be a good fit for your business. Otherwise, your marketing will be too broad and generalised, and won't have the power to connect.

One of the first concepts to accept is that you don't need to please everyone. For that matter, you really don't *want* to please everyone. You want your marketing to *really* connect with a niche group. When I say *really connect*, I mean it speaks to them in a way that makes them feel your company was made just for them.

A notable example is phones. On the surface, an iPhone and an Android can both do pretty much the same things. They make calls, take photos, play music and have millions of apps to choose from. Yet there are two distinct customer camps. Within these groups, you've got a range, varying from the hardcore advocates through to the indifferent. The hardcore clan will only buy the brand they are loyal to; those on the more indifferent end of the scale can be swayed if you give them a good enough reason (eg price or convenience).

From a marketing point of view, it's easier and more powerful to focus on your advocates or those who are most likely to buy from you. And if that marketing catches some others from the periphery, great. When it comes to knowing your ideal customer, this is really getting to know your hardcore advocates.

So, the question begs, how do you find your ideal customer? A good starting point is to look at your current customers and examine them using the 80/20 principle. Who are the 20 per cent of your current customers who are bringing in 80 per cent of your revenue or profit? Go over your customer list and find out who is spending money with you.

It can be tedious work, but it will pay dividends. If you take the time to find out exactly who brings you the most business, you can then focus on like-minded clientele. Marketing to specific clientele will both increase the impact of your marketing and reduce your marketing costs, as you will not have to market on such a large scale.

Of course, sales volume is not the only measure of a great client (and can even be one that leads you astray). Some other characteristics to consider are:

- the type of work they give you (see the section on core competency) – this is often linked to the profitability of the customer
- the frequency of work – for example, one massive order per year that chokes production or steady amounts throughout the year
- convenience – their geography or communication style
- service needs – high maintenance or smooth and easy
- enjoyment factor – do you and your team like working with them? (Don't underestimate this one.)

If you are just starting out and don't have customers yet, this is the time for you to decide who you want to target and work with, and who your business is truly intended for.

Truthfully, it may take winning some customers for you

to get really clear on that, but starting with your best guess will give you some direction and make some decisions easier to make. Through the process of working with different customers, you'll get some contrast, and armed with the knowledge of your ideal customer, you'll start to see where the fit is.

As you spend some time pondering the above points, you should start to see some patterns emerge. You might start to see that your customers fall into categories. Ideally, through this process, you'll end up with one to three categories of customers that you can then write a detailed avatar about, describing each as if they were individual customers.

For example, in our business, SalesUp! Business Coaching, we have three distinct categories:
1. Owners of businesses that are growing (possibly very quickly) who want to make sure they scale the growth correctly and not have it consume them.
2. Owners of businesses who want growth but are not growing.
3. Owners of businesses that are in trouble and need a turnaround. (This is a very small part of our market and taking them on is very dependent on the qualities of the owner[s].)

We also have two main company types we work with: professional services and manufacturing. At any one time, we may select a specific industry within these to focus our marketing efforts, depending on what we feel is appropriate or relevant at the time.

> Within each of these categories, we have a detailed avatar describing the actual person (their values, interests, skills etc). We've based these on actual clients rather than fictional clients because we find this much easier. For us, the qualities and characteristics of the owner are critical. Depending on who your ideal customer is, that may be equally or less important.

Perhaps you already have a customer or two from each of your identified categories who exemplifies your ideal customer. If so, use them as your avatar. This means that when you are thinking about attracting more of that category of customer, you are targeting your marketing efforts at your avatar.

For a guide on determining your ideal customer avatars, visit our resource centre for a complete walkthrough tool.
jumpingoffthewheel.com

What problem are you solving?

Now that you know who your ideal customer is, we need to understand exactly which of their problems you are solving through your business. This might be easy to answer on the surface, but I want you to think about it the way your customer thinks about it. What language do they use? And further, what are the deeper issues that don't always get spoken about?

Let's use an example: we'll take a printer as we've worked with quite a few over the years. On the outset, it would be fair to say the problem printers solve is getting stuff printed, and I would agree with that assessment. But if that was the only problem, then someone who needs printing would just go to the first printer they found and say, 'Can you please print this?' Of course, that sometimes happens, but for some other print buyers, there's more to it. Here are some subsections of print buyers.

1. Some print buyers are very concerned about price. They just need something printed. As long as the quality is right and the timing fair, they want the lowest price they can find (eg direct mail flyers). Their problem is financial. They are trying to minimise costs.

2. For some print buyers, the biggest problem is quality. They need to reproduce their images within quality ranges that you typically won't get from your local copy shop. If the quality is lacking, it will affect their brand and reputation (eg photographic reproductions and premium brands). Their problem is brand consistency and protecting their reputation.

3. For other print buyers, timing is critical. They may be coordinating in-store promotions or a product launch that matches with TV advertising, and if it's a day late, it would be a complete disaster. Their problem is turnaround times and dependability.

4. Another type of print buyer might have very complex needs but be very understaffed within their own company, so they are looking for a printer who can help them be organised and efficient (eg national retail chains). Their problem is logistics and resources.

5. And still another may want a wide variety of items printed and needs a printer with diverse abilities and expert knowledge. Their problem is knowledge and making diverse buying easy.

So, you see, just within this one example, we've quickly been able to identify five core problems these print buyers may be looking to solve.

Another way to think about what problems someone might have is to think about what concerns they have when they need to buy what your company provides. What risks or problems will keep them up at night? What could cause them to look bad in the minds of their boss/customer?

With that in mind, if you are a printer and marketing yourself as a printer who prints anything for anyone, you will most likely end up in the price category because there is no clear value-added problem that you solve.

Using our example, think back to the ideal customer and how the type of customer you have will vary, depending on what the problem is. It is worth noting that it is unlikely your ideal customer will match all five of these problems.

Sticking with the above example, when you choose to excel in one of these five areas, you will now resonate with a smaller niche of print customers, which is great. It means you can speak their language and you only need to speak one language. You can get good at doing and speaking about that one thing so that anyone who has that problem will know you are the person to go and see.

You will stand out loud and clear compared to the printer who can do it all, regardless of the fact they may be able to do what you can do. The power is in the messaging to the customer or prospect, and how they perceive you versus your competition.

Never try to solve all five of these problems to appeal to a larger audience. This is a classic mistake business owners and marketers make. They think, 'Well, I can solve all those problems, so I should, and then I'll have a bigger pool of customers to draw from, and our business will be so much bigger.' This is faulty thinking and it can really hurt your business.

Consider this example I saw recently. I witnessed a woman talking about her own business, which was running mastermind groups. The way she talked about them was compelling. It was clear she knew what she was talking about and, from the sounds of what she had to say, was having a lot of success with her clients. When she had finished talking about this she said, 'Oh, and I also sell these hand-made greeting cards, which I paint myself.' What thoughts would run through your mind at that moment?

Truthfully, if I had looked at the cards without knowing anything else about her, I would have been impressed by the cards, but something in my mind didn't fit with the mastermind facilitator-cum-greeting-card artist. It just didn't fit. Now, she may well be world class at both things, but the message was confusing to the audience, and you could see people switch off.

Imagine if Apple began making golf clubs. Some people might buy them, but it is unlikely Apple is ever going to dominate the golf club market. It just doesn't fit.

The same goes for the printer who can produce the highest quality in record time, distribute nationally and solve complex logistics, while also having the most competitive price. People have a tough time believing it can be done (regardless of whether it can be), so they may discount the claim. They may not even do it consciously. They may not know why they gravitate toward a specialist, but they do.

Another good example is health practitioners who say they can fix everything. Now, they may well be able to, but the potential patient's brain says, 'Mmm … I don't think so,' and doubt sets in. Once doubt is the first impression, it's very hard to change.

These health practitioners are better off picking a specialty. I mean, who would have heart surgery from the surgeon who also pulls teeth?

What are you good at?

This may seem like a strange question, but it's one well worth considering. Just like our points in the previous section, there can be a strong tendency to want to be good at everything. But the truth is, you aren't, and you don't want to be. No one is good at everything.

Companies that are leading their industries decide what areas to be intentionally bad at so they can be out-of-this-world in other areas. And guess what? The areas they are amazingly good at are the areas their customers care most about, and the areas they are intentionally bad at are way lower on their customers' value radar.

To do this, it comes back to being super clear on who your ideal customers are because your ideal customers will have a different set of values from the other potential customers. Think back to our printer example. How could our printer be exceptionally good at complex logistics and delivery deadlines, and have the most competitive price? It would be very hard to do, and I suspect the customer who values the complex logistics and delivery guarantees is willing to sacrifice in terms of price.

Back to you. We've established that you are not good at everything (perhaps a better word is great) and should at least be on the road to being okay with that. Now, let's look at what you *are* great at. To do this, consider the distinct categories of work or customers you have. There is no right way to segment your work here. We are attempting to distill down to your most core competency. Here are some key questions to ponder as you work it out.

1. What type of work is the most profitable for you? Refer to your P&L to help you. Hopefully, you can segment your income and costs by type of work. If you can't, this is something to consider for the future.
2. What type of work do you and your team enjoy the most?
3. What type of work is easiest for your team to process and deliver on?
4. In what area(s) does your company have the most knowledge?
5. In what area(s) do you and your team have the greatest interest?
6. What type of work are you best known for?

Now, have a look at how well the answers match up with your ideal customer's problems. Where is the fit?

Hopefully, there is a fit, and if not, you might need to go back and rework both sections. By the completion of this exercise, your goal is to have alignment between what you are great at and your ideal customer's core problems that you can solve.

Your competition

'Keep your friends close and your enemies closer.' Wise advice from *The Godfather*.

The next part of the puzzle is taking a close look at your competitors. Only by knowing your competition are you able to complete the last step of your marketing blueprint, which is how to present yourself as different.

If you don't know who your competitors are, it's time to engage the mother-load of information on the internet. Search for them. You can also ask your customers and prospects, if appropriate.

Here are some things you might want to know.

1. What do they claim is unique about them?
2. What promises are they making?
3. Who appears to be their target market (ideal customer)?
4. What sort of marketing are they doing and where?
5. What is their web/social media presence like?
6. How are they different from your company?
7. How much momentum and mass do they have? By that, I mean how long they've been around, how big they are and how well they're known. Put more simply: are they a nobody or a somebody?

(*Note*: while I advocate getting to know who your competition is, once you've done that, I believe in keeping your focus on your business, not theirs. There is a well-known principle that what you focus on grows, so if you are spending unnecessary time and effort focused on what your competitors are doing, that is energy taken away from your own business. Obviously, there is a balance here; you don't want to be naïve, but hopefully, you get my point.)

Be different – what is your unique selling proposition

This last piece of your marketing blueprint is the pinnacle, the Holy Grail, and the cornerstone of your marketing efforts. It's *almost* not worth doing any marketing until you've got this part sorted because you may end up wasting a lot of time and money on marketing that will be less effective.

Your USP is how you are going to communicate to your ideal customer why they should choose you. It will underpin all your marketing efforts.

There is no secret formula for developing your USP. If there were, there would be more companies doing a better job in this area. The fact is, it does take a bit of work. And this is great news for you because it means most people don't do it, most likely including your competition.

There are two main forms a USP can take:

1. a claim or claims that differentiate you from your competition
2. a guarantee.

The need for a USP is dependent on the level of competition you have. If you are carving a niche in a new industry, your challenge is less about direct competition and more about the lack of awareness and value.

If, however, you are in a very mature and saturated industry like, say, plumbing, a USP will be critical.

The basis of your USP will stem from the work you've already done around your ideal customer, the problem they have, your core competencies and your competition. Some other questions to consider include the following.

- What are the perceived standards of your industry? (Think customer service, technology, and quality.)

- What annoys customers about your industry?
- What would you have to do to get your ideal customers saying to their friends and associates that they'd be crazy not to use [your company]?

As you throw around all these thoughts and get them down on paper (or up on a whiteboard), you'll start to get a glimpse of where the intersection lies between what your customers value, what you're good at and how you're different from your competition.

Once you've got the essence of it, you can spend more time (or engage an outside resource) to help you do the copywriting.

When it comes to a guarantee, think about the emotional risks your ideal customer may perceive when it comes to buying from you for the first time. For example, a hairdressing client of ours worked out that the perceived risk for their prospective clients was that the stylist would screw it up and make them look like a fool. So, they came up with the following guarantee: 'We guarantee you'll get more compliments from friends and family after seeing us than you've ever had after seeing another stylist.'

This is an interesting example; how do you measure that? Hard, right? But that's not the point. The point is that the guarantee addressed the primary perceived emotional risk the ideal customer felt and helped put them at ease enough for them to give the salon a try.

You may be able to see from this example that sometimes a perceived risk is not always at the conscious level of your potential customer's thoughts. This is where you must get inside your customer's head as best you can and attempt to think the way they would think.

(*Note*: the hairdresser didn't need to offer a money-back guarantee or, even worse, offer a satisfaction guarantee. Those types of guarantees are way too common, and therefore come across with very little power. Your guarantee needs to smack someone between the eyes and hit their emotional concerns head on.)

An example of where a money-back guarantee has worked well is a client of ours who owns a used-car business. In that industry, the perceived risk of getting scammed is prolific. In response, our client put in writing what they were willing to do if someone was not happy – an unequivocal 30-day, no-questions-asked, money-back guarantee. And yes, they were very nervous about trying that guarantee, but as is most often the case, their fears were unfounded.

Get in touch with how first-time customers feel and what concerns they have before they make a purchase. If you can alleviate the fears they may have with a guarantee (and back it up with testimonials), you'll go a long way to cutting through the competitive noise in the marketplace.

Examples of USPs include:

- services:
    - Chem-Dry carpet cleaning: Drier, Cleaner, Healthier
    - FedEx: When it absolutely positively has to be there overnight
    - Avis: We're number two, we try harder
    - Domino's Pizza: Delivered in 30 minutes or it's free
- products:
    - M&M's: The milk chocolate that melts in your mouth, not in your hand

- Dyson hand dryers: Fastest, most hygienic and costs less to run
- Bridge Road Brewery's Pale Ale: Voted #1 in Victoria.

THE 6-POINT GROWTH MODEL

The 6-point growth model is a model for growing your sales and profits. The 6 points refer to the points you can proactively work on to achieve that growth. Those 6 points are:

- lead generation
- conversion rate
- customer retention
- customer spend
- gross margins
- fixed costs or overhead.

Figure 7 shows you the overall picture of the 6-point growth model.

- Your sales are driven by your number of customers (total customers) and how much they spend on average (spend per customer).
- Your number of customers (total customers) is affected by your number of repeat customers and new customers.
- Your number of repeat customers is driven by your retention rate of past customers.
- Your number of new customers is determined by leads generated and your conversion rate.

The shade coding indicates:

■ lighter grey boxes are results – they cannot be directly influenced by you

■ darker grey boxes are influencers – they can be influenced by you.

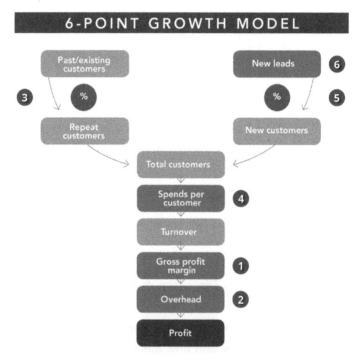

FIGURE 7: THE 6-POINT GROWTH MODEL

In the Money section, we covered your profit model. Your profit model showed the allocation of expenses and profit, relative to your sales. Think of your profit model as having 2 points (margins and overhead). The 6-point model adds another 4 points to it (lead generation, conversion rate, customer retention, customer spend).

The two models break down like this:

- growing sales – 4 points
- keeping profit – 2 points (profit model).

We've already spent quite a bit of time getting clear on profitability, so let's now turn our attention to growing the top-line sales. In this section, we are going to focus on the 4 points that grow sales:

1. lead generation
2. conversion rate
3. retention rate
4. average spend per customer.

Growing your sales can be difficult, to say the least. I mean, where do you start? Is it a case of needing more customers, or is it better to focus on servicing the ones you have and getting them to buy more? Possibly, it's a combination of both.

Let's say you do need more customers. Is it your lead generation that needs boosting, or do you need to be doing a better job of converting those leads into sales?

As you can see from the preliminary questions above, knowing where to start is an important first step. We tend to see lots of examples of people who want to grow their sales and so head straight into spending money on marketing and advertising. While there are times this is the right approach, most of the time it's not.

But first, to help you fully understand the power of this simple model, let's put in some numbers.

The model is relatively straightforward, but be warned – it's just a model. When you run your numbers through, it may not be perfect, and it's not supposed to be. It's intended to guide you on where your opportunities might lie and what is possible.

6-POINT GROWTH MODEL

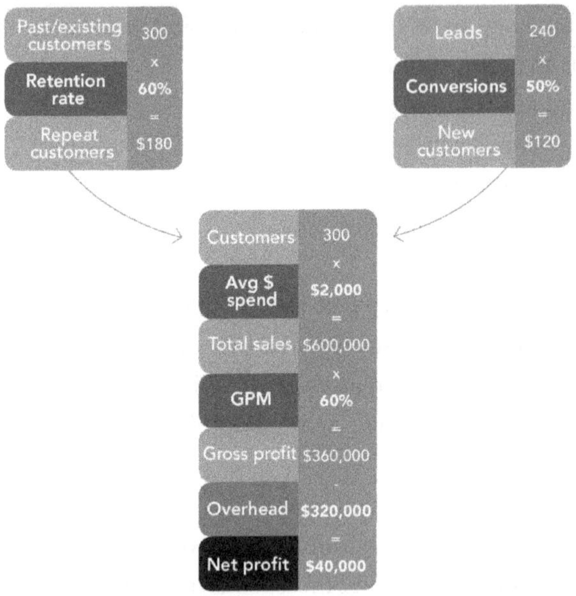

FIGURE 8: A 6-POINT NUMBERS GRAPHIC

To give you a quick explanation of what all this means:

- the sample business in Figure 8 has 300 past customers who bought from it in the previous year(s)
- of those 300 customers, 60 per cent will buy again in the following year, giving it 180 repeat customers
- its marketing generates 240 leads or enquiries over the year

- it converts 50 per cent of those enquiries into customers, which gives it 120 new customers throughout the year
- adding together repeat customers and new customers, it had a total customer count of 300 customers (180 repeats + 120 new)
- on average, its customers spend $2,000 over the course of the year (some will spend more than others, but on average, it will be $2,000)
- multiplying out the total number of customers and the average spend; its total sales are $600,000 (300 x $2,000)
- it has a gross profit margin of 60 per cent, which gives it a gross profit of $360,000 ($600,000 x 60 per cent)
- its overhead for the year is $320,000
- this leaves it with $40,000 of profit ($360,000 – $320,000).

Note: To download a blank template for you to input your own numbers, see our resource section.
jumpingoffthewheel.com

Once populated, the model should start to make a little more sense. Where it really gets interesting is when we start tweaking the numbers. Let's try that out. For the purposes of this example, and to show you how small changes in the 6-point growth model can have dramatic effects on your profitability, here is the model again in Figure 9, but this time we have made the following changes:

1. increase lead generation by 10 per cent

2. increase conversion rate by 10 per cent
3. increase retention by 10 per cent
4. increase spend per customer by 10 per cent
5. increase gross margin by 5 per cent
6. decrease overhead by 5 per cent.

Later in this chapter, I'll share our top five strategies on how you can generate those improvements in your own business.

You can see with some slight changes, we've grown:

- the number of customers by 14.4 per cent
- the sales by 25 per cent
- profitability by a whopping 300+ per cent.

So, slight changes, when compounded, can make a massive difference.

Of course, every business is different, so the examples here must be taken in the context of your business. Be sure to extract the principles behind the gains and apply them in a relevant way to your business.

This model is helpful in allowing you to see how you are doing today, and more importantly, where the opportunities may lie to help you hit your growth targets.

There are two ways to use this model.

1. Run your numbers as they are today, then look for the best opportunities within the 6-point model to grow your business. Apply some conservative improvements and see what could be.

2. Set sales and profitability targets for where you want to be and work backwards. For a real-life example of this, see the case study, The 6-point growth model in action: working backwards on the following pages.

6-POINT GROWTH MODEL

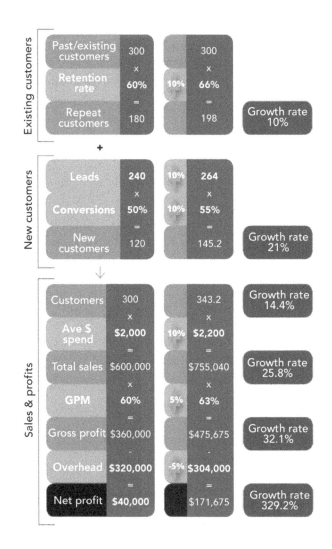

FIGURE 9: AN IMPROVED 6-POINT GROWTH MODEL

Building out the model as you would like it to be and comparing it to what you have today allows you to see where your opportunities are, and subsequently, where to focus your efforts.

It also helps you understand the magnitude of effort you need to apply to reach your goal. Invariably, when we've had clients complete this exercise, they have one of two possible reactions.

1. 'Wow, it won't be that hard to make that happen ... awesome!'
2. 'Wow, we need to put in some serious work to make that happen.'

Either way, you now have an objective picture of what needs doing, and you will no longer be operating from a place of wishful thinking. Too often, people set lofty growth goals without a clear picture of what is required to make them happen. This inevitably leads to delusion, followed quickly by disappointment.

(*Note*: Seeing the model is one thing, but creating the plan to make it happen is another. See A 90-day plan section. Executing your plan is yet another again. See the Execution and rhythm section.)

The 6-point growth model in action
1: working backwards

Yvonne wanted to build a $1 million legal business inside the next 3 years. She was currently sitting at $264,000 in annual sales and was at just about break even for profitability (after paying herself a good salary), so this was no small goal.

Our starting point was to work out what her 6-point model currently looked like. To do that, we worked out her average spend per client, and retention and conversion rates, which were:

- retention rate – 48 per cent
- conversion rate – 77 per cent
- average spend per customer – $1791.

Then, using her number of clients and total sales, we could build her current model.

Now that we had the current model, we needed to tweak the numbers over a 3-year period to get them to produce a $1 million revenue business.

(*Note*: while Yvonne was focused on top-line growth, rest assured we also helped her to be focused on profitability. Remember, focusing only on top-line growth can be a suicide mission.)

Figure 10 shows how we built out that model. You can see from the model, we played around with some numbers until we reached our target and had the variables at a point that made some sense.

- Retention increase by 5 per cent each year.
- Lead generation increase by 32 per cent each year (this is obviously the big one).
- Conversion rate increase by 5 per cent in the first year and 3 per cent for the following 2 years (this was already high, so further gains may be more difficult).
- Average spend to increase by 20 per cent year over year (this is also a big target).
- There are no changes to gross profit margin because all her labour costs are captured in overhead. Here, gross profit margin is determined by disbursements

such as search fees and so on. These likely won't change.

- Overhead has increased quite a bit, and this is mainly labour. At each level of sales volume, we had worked out how many she'd need on her team and what that would cost.

6-POINT GROWTH MODEL

			Year 1		Year 2		Year 3	
Existing customers	Past/existing customers	148		147.9		180.8		240.1
	×			×		×		×
	Retention rate	48.6%	5%	51.03%	5%	53.58%	5%	56.26%
	=			=		=		=
	Repeat customers	71.9		75.5		96.9		135.1
				+		+		+
New customers	Leads	100	32%	132	32%	174.2	32%	230
	×			×		×		×
	Conversions	76%	5%	80%	3%	82%	3%	85%
	=			=		=		=
	New customers	76		105.336		143.215		194.715
				↓		↓		↓
Sales & profits	Customers	147.9		180.8		240.1		329.8
	×			×		×		×
	Ave $ spend	$1,791	20%	$2,149	20%	$2,579	20%	$3,095
	=			=		=		=
	Total sales	$264,939		$386,626		$619,235		$1,020,675
	×			×		×		×
	GPM	86%	0%	86%	0%	86%	0%	86%
	=			=		=		=
	Gross profit	$227,848		$334,219		$532,542		$877,781
	Overhead	$225,000	20%	$270,000	30%	$351,000	40%	$491,400
	=			=		=		=
	Net profit	$2,848		$64,219		$181,542		$386,381

FIGURE 10: YVONNE'S 6-POINT MODEL

Completing this exercise gave Yvonne a clear picture of where the focus needed to be, and she could also now see how much work was going to be involved.

While there was a lot of work to do, at least she knew that going in. There was no head in the sand, hoping things would grow. From here, we helped her choose some very specific strategies to work on in the first year. This was further broken down into 90-day segments, allowing her to focus on just one or two areas at a time, which helped her stay focused and avoid overwhelm.

The 6-point growth model in action
2: natural consequences of knowing the numbers

You met Jacky and Jason earlier when we talked about testing and measuring your marketing. We saw how the impact of some simple measuring gave them insights on how their marketing dollars were working (or not, in their case).

Our next step in working with them was to show them how measuring the numbers in other areas could have a similar impact.

We showed the team the 6-point growth model and they latched onto it immediately. They identified that the key drivers for them were: leads, conversion and average spend. They set up a dashboard and started measuring religiously.

Results came fast and without what seemed like a whole lot of effort. As they progressed, they saw their conversion rate start to climb. When it plateaued, it sparked a conversation around objection handling and positioning. Brainstorming ideas became a natural consequence to keep the needle moving in the right direction.

When they came to look at average customer spend (which they converted to gross profit per sale), it caused them to closely examine their sweet spot, which they worked out was cars valued between $7000 and $12,000. Anything more and they were turning more dollars but not generating significantly more gross profit (which had negative effects on their cash flow as their inventory value was higher).

The key takeaway for them was that simply measuring the key drivers raised their awareness of what was driving their business, and naturally caused them to explore their actions in influencing these numbers.

In addition, we implemented a variety of strategies that kept the numbers climbing, but the power was in the foundational principles of measuring and having raised awareness. If you don't know what the numbers are, it's impossible to improve them.

As Peter Drucker famously said, 'What gets measured gets managed.'

Making it work for you

So, how do you make this 6-point growth model work for you? We follow a 5-step process outlined below.

Step 1 Measure your numbers as they are today.

Step 2 Set your profit goal and work the numbers backwards until you get it to a point you believe is achievable.

Step 3 Develop a series of 90-day plans (see the Planning section) complete with the strategies and actions you will take to improve your key drivers.

Be aware when it comes to execution, there is a pre-ferred order to approach the 6 points, which will again vary depending on your business and your current situation (ie a mature business will most probably have a different optimised order from a start-up). The order goes as follows.

1. *Overheads* – cutting overheads is the quickest path to profit. But you can only cut so far. It's about being lean and efficient. Never grow sales to compensate for lazy cost management.

2. *Margins* – these are also about efficiency and finding your sweet spot. Many strategies here cost nothing to implement and can bring immediate results.

3. *Retention* – stop the leaks before adding more customers. This one may sometimes be the priority, and it can also be the last depending on the current state of the business.

4. *Average customer spend* – low-cost strategies can be implemented with quick results.

5. *Conversion rate* – it is better to optimise this before investing in generating more leads.

6. *Lead generation* – this is listed last because it's the beginning of the model and often the most resource intensive to implement in terms of time and money. when you optimise the other 5 points first, any money then spent on lead generation will earn a much higher return.

Step 4 Execute with relentless rhythm, all the while measuring your numbers and keeping track of your progress. Remember, what gets measured gets managed.

Step 5 Review, refine and repeat.

A note on measuring

The way you measure each of the 6 points will depend on what data systems you already have in your business. The ideal solution – and something to work toward if you don't have it – is a CRM (customer relationship management software) or similar system that tracks all your prospects and customer activity.

If you are not at that stage (and most are not), start as simply as possible with the things you can measure. Getting into the habit is the priority. Once the habit is created, and you can see the value in having the information, you can then look at how you can make it easier, and ideally, automatic to collate.

You don't want to end up with 16 spreadsheets to review every month. Devoting that kind of time just won't realistically happen. Pick the easiest of the 6 drivers for you to measure, start measuring them, then add the next driver, and so on.

Involving your team

Some of the standard reactions we've seen when clients ask their employees to start measuring stuff varies from defensiveness (they mistake it to be about monitoring and micro-managing them) to apathy. Change requires effort. It's vitally important you educate your team as to *why* it's important that the business measures things.

I'm a huge fan of transparency and open-book management (see the Targets and sharing information section for more). To that end, I would highly encourage you to share the 6-point growth model with your team. When people have all the information, and understand why it is important, they are empowered to make better choices. They also feel trusted.

Educate them on 'what gets measured gets managed'. A great analogy here is weight loss. Anyone who has ever tried will know that stepping on the scale is a key part of sticking with behaviour changes related to eating because it raises awareness. You want to do the same with your team. You want them to be conscious of their actions, so the company can be proactive in growth.

It's critical to get employee buy-in to build a more financially healthy business. In case you are not sure of the benefits to the team, here's a shortlist:

- job security
- job advancement opportunity
- funds to invest in the right equipment
- funds to invest in training
- ability to better compensate those who add more value (not across-the-board pay rises)
- ability to better compete with a stronger marketing presence
- ability to weather any downturns (which brings it all back to job security).

The strength and flavour of your company's culture will have a direct impact on how well your team responds (see the Playing rules section under the 4 Ps of People for more.)

Measuring leads

As mentioned, this is ideally done by your CRM software. If you don't have that ability, then some form of manual recording will be necessary. If you do have a CRM system, ensure it's being used correctly. You want to be able to extract reports showing:

- number of leads generated during various periods
- source of the lead (ie which form of marketing brought it in: referral, website, flyer, etc.)

A manual system can be a simple spreadsheet showing the date, some details of the lead (name, company, etc.) and the source.

Measuring conversion rate

Once you measure leads effectively, measuring conversation rate is straightforward. Of your leads, which ones became customers? Again, ideally, you would have a CRM system that can do this for you (so long as the data is being entered correctly). If you don't have a CRM system, use your lead tracking forms to track manually. Add a column or two in your lead tracking form to indicate if the enquiry (lead) became a sale.

Be sure to include dates for your lead and conversion rate tracking. An important strategy for improving conversion rate is to reduce your sales cycle time (ie the time between when a lead is generated and when they become a customer). This can only be tweaked if you are able to measure your sales cycle time. Specifically, you want to know the date a lead is created and the date the first sale is made. The difference between these dates is your sales cycle.

Retention rate

This can be one of the harder ones to measure if you don't have the systems to generate the data. As you start to generate some historical data (or perhaps you have it already) you can then look at retention rate. To make it easy for our clients (and you), I've created a retention rate calculator tool you are welcome to download from the companion site jumpingoffthewheel.com. You really need two or three periods (see the Notes on using the retention calculator section to work out what duration your period should be) to be able to get a good handle on retention rate. Figure 11 gives you a snapshot of how to calculate your retention rate.

The two variables you need to be able to measure and input are:

- A – total of unique customers for a period
- B – new customers for the same period.

The calculator will do the rest.

	Period 1	Period 2	Period 3	Period 4	Period 5	Period 6
A – Total unique # customers	1000	1200	1300	1450	1500	1450
B – New customers for period	300	250	200	300	200	200
C – Existing customers for period	700	950	1100	1150	1300	1250
D – # Lost customers for prior period		50	100	150	150	250
Retention rate		95.0%	91.7%	88.5%	89.7%	83.3%

FIGURE 11: RETENTION RATE CALCULATOR

You can see from Figure 11 that it would be easy for this company to get excited by its growth in customers (and no doubt sales). Yes, it had a small downturn in period 6 (growth is rarely a straight line), but overall, the trend looks up. Yet when we look at its retention rate, we see a different story.

Clearly, it is having issues keeping its customers happy as it grows. Or, perhaps its marketing is bringing in the wrong type of leads and the new customers are not sticking. Either way, this trend highlights a problem this company needs to fix if it's going to continue sustainable growth. Some more exploration is required to get to the bottom of the problem.

To download this calculator, visit our resource section.
jumpingoffthewheel.com

The calculator gives some interesting trends and information, such as:

- how is your customer base trending?
- how is your retention rate trending?
- how is your lead generation trending?
- is your lead generation outpacing your retention by a healthy margin, ie are you bringing in more customers than you are losing?

NOTES ON USING THE RETENTION CALCULATOR

- To determine the best length of time for a period in the calculation, you need to be aware of the repeat buying cycle for your customers. If customers typically buy four or five times a year, I would use a quarterly period. If they buy once or twice a year, I would perhaps use an 18-month period. Choose a period that is longer than the repeat buying cycle, and it will make your numbers more accurate.

- Period 1 is your starting point and won't give you any usable information, but you do need it as your benchmark.
- The retention rate is calculated by comparing the number of existing customers over a period to the total number of customers for the previous period. This calculates the number of lost customers as a percentage of total customers (for the previous period). If that confuses you too much, just download the calculator (jumpingoffthewheel.com).

Measuring average customer spend

Again, we are back to your CRM or invoicing system. You need to have the ability to track the number of unique customers that bought from you during any period. This is *not* the total number of sales transactions because some customers will have bought more than once.

Once you know the number of unique customers for a period, simply divide your sales for that period by the number of unique customers in the same period.

average spend per customer = total sales/number of unique customers

Measuring gross margin

This will come from your accounting system and should be straightforward. You might need to revisit how your chart of accounts (how costs are categorised in your accounting software) is set up to give you meaningful data. If you're unclear on this, speak with your accountant. If your accountant looks at you strangely, look for another accountant.

(*Note*: many accountants are great at tax preparation and associated topics. Tweaking your chart of accounts is more of a management accounting function, not a tax accounting function, and not all accountants are as proficient in this area.

Measuring overheads

Just like gross margin percentage, this will come straight from your accounting system.

The 20 per cent growth strategies (our top 5)

Now let's get into the fun stuff – how you can be proactive with the 6 points to get your sales and profits growing.

Before we get into it, a quick disclaimer. This book is not intended to be a comprehensive guide to all the marketing and sales strategies you can choose from. That said, we do have our go-to strategies that are usually (notice I said *usually* and not *always*) the first stop when we look to leveraging the growth model with our clients.

Our full toolbox that contains 186 strategies which have varying degrees of value and applicability, and they are customised for our clients depending on the business and stage of growth. But to get an idea, we'll share with you here our top 5 strategies for each of the 6 points.

As we go through these, bear this in mind: what is right for you will depend on the growth stage of your business, your skill sets and natural talents (and those of your team), and the resources you have available (time and money).

 For a more comprehensive list, download our marketing vehicle checklist from our resources section.
jumpingoffthewheel.com

LEADS
Referral system

Referrals are perhaps one of the best known, but most underutilised, strategies for building a business. That said, most people are using referrals as their number 1 strategy, but they would more likely call it word of mouth versus referrals. If you are getting word of mouth, that is great. In fact, it may be quite a problem if you are not.

Just be aware there is a difference between receiving unsolicited word of mouth referrals and having a proactive strategy to help your customers refer you.

Before you embark on a proactive referral strategy, there is one golden rule you must abide by – be referable.

- Your customers need to love working with you and your team.
- You need to deliver consistent results for your customers.
- You must be professional. (ie be well presented, do what you say you will do, be on time etc.)
- Provide more value than your customers expect. Be able to deliver the wow factor.

People are generally willing to refer when they've had an outstanding experience with your company. They *may* refer when they've had a satisfactory experience, and they likely *won't* refer when they've had an average or below average experience.

It's also helpful to keep in mind that each customer is different. Some will refer more easily than others simply because some people get a kick out of helping people, and they are more social and connected.

Your biggest obstacle in being referred is the perceived risk associated with referring to you. A question in the potential referrer's mind is, 'Am I going to look good or bad in the eyes of the person I'm referring?' They are thinking (consciously or unconsciously) how this referral will affect their reputation.

Those decisions are all based on their experience and the perceptions created by that experience. No amount of bribing will be able to convince someone to refer if they don't feel safe in doing so.

There are four common mechanisms for generating referrals. Which ones you use will depend on your type of business and the type of relationship you have with your clients.

1. Referral gift: if you provide a referral you get _____ and your referee gets _____.
2. Competition draw: enter your name, plus two of your friends to win _____. This can work equally well on Facebook: like our page and go into the draw to win _____.
3. Promote an event: this is a very low-threat strategy that also gives value. Your event must be perceived as valuable. When people promote, and their friends sign up, you get to start the relationship. Have an offer at the end of your event that is applicable (eg a hairdresser may run an in-house session on make-up skills with an offer for some product or an extra free service when booking a haircut).
    a. Promote by giving 'you plus a friend' invitations to your customers; ask customers to retweet/repost; ask customers to send an email invitation to five friends etc.

b. This works well for webinars. It's easy to forward an invitation to a webinar. Then, after the webinar, you can have people comment and share through your Facebook fan page. (*Note*: webinars typically have a very low conversion rate, so plan accordingly.)

4. Straight out ask: this method needs to be done at the right time (eg when customers are happy with something you've done for them) and you must have earned it. This can work well for businesses that get to know their customers well. Be specific about who you want them to refer. Don't ask an open-ended question like, 'Who do you know?' That is asking them to review (usually on the spot) every single person they know. Instead, guide them with, 'Who do you know who is _____ and _____ and looking to _____?'

It can help to position the client when you first start the relationship for example, ('Bob, when we get going and you are stoked with all the excellent work we've done for you, would you be comfortable if at that point, I was to ask you for an introduction to a couple of your connections, who you feel may be a good fit for what we do?')

This position is non-threatening in the moment but plants the seed and allows you to ask them to refer down the track, once you've earned it. When you do, it won't be a surprise or out of place. 'Bob, remember when we started, I asked you ...?'

Strategic alliances
A strategic alliance (SA) is a partnership between two or more businesses that share the same ideal customers but do

not directly compete. This partnership is established by leveraging each other to generate new leads for each business. SAs can be one of the most powerful of all marketing strategies. They can also be one of the hardest to get working well.

When talking with business owners, it's a common occurrence that they have tried to set them up, but they never really amounted to anything or just fizzled out. Hence the need for a proven methodology to create partnerships that work. Lucky for you, that's what this section is all about, so read on.

So why are SAs so cool? Think about it this way – if you could find five other businesses with hundreds of customers who were your ideal customers, and they agreed to promote your business to their customers, what impact could that have on your business? How much do you think that would cost you to do versus paid advertising, either online or via traditional vehicles like newspapers?

When a lead is generated from an SA, it's a form of referral. And referrals come with a degree of inferred trust. The level of trust varies depending on the depth of the relationship between the SA and the customer, but regardless, trust helps with conversion.

So, how do you get all these businesses to promote you and send you free leads? Let's ask the question a different way: what would someone have to do for you to promote their business to your customers? There you have the crux of the concept. A sustainable SA is one where *both* parties benefit, and the level of perceived benefit is equal and fair.

There are six key steps to getting an SA up and running.
Step 1 Know your ideal customer(s) and choose one of your avatars.

Step 2 Brainstorm potential SA partners – download our SA wheel to make this easy for you. See below.

Step 3 Make contact. Start with people you already have relationships with. Just like referrals, SAs require trust, which takes time to build.

Step 4 Filter through your process. Of all the people you contact, you'll find some are all over it, some will just talk the talk, and some just won't get it or aren't interested. *You only want those who are as passionate about it as you are.*

Step 5 The finalists. As you execute step 4, a few contenders will rise to the top. Eliminate the rest and put all your focus on these few. Remember 80/20.

Step 6 Execute. Through your meetings, you will have established some action steps and ideas on how to work together. Get your teams involved and plan out some specific action plans to make the partnership a reality.

For a detailed guide on setting up strategic alliances that work, see the resource section of our website. There you can also download the SA wheel.
jumpingoffthewheel.com

Networking

It's not who you know – it's who knows you. And to take it one step further, it's who knows you *and* trusts you. Just like with referrals and SAs, having a strong network that trusts you is invaluable.

I learned this when we moved back to Australia from Canada. After running my business for 11 years in Canada, I took for granted the strong network I'd developed, not only as a referral source, but also businesses I could refer others to. When we moved, I realised how powerful that network was because now I didn't have one that was local.

It amazes me how often I meet businesspeople who are not networked and connected. They say the strength of your network shows up in the value of your net worth. While this may be a little clichéd, I think the saying has some merit. The best sales people are the ones with the best networks, not the best cold callers.

Join groups, clubs and associations to get involved. There are formal networking groups like BNI, and there are less formal approaches such as helping with a charity. Whatever your flavour, it's critical to mix, mingle and get connected with others who are connected and in a growth mindset.

Your circles of influence (your network) will have three layers.

1. *Inner circle*: those who know and trust you implicitly. These will be your best customers (top 20 per cent), close friends (hopefully), family and your A-level strategic partners.

2. *Mid circle*: your B-level strategic partners will be here, as well as the remainder of your customer base. It will also comprise others in your network who you know reasonably well, but don't have formal strategic partnerships with.

3. *Outer circle*: those who know you but have a very limited relationship with you. Think of those acquaintances you see out and about and know each other to say hello to, but that is about it.

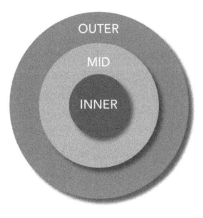

FIGURE 12: NETWORK CIRCLES

Draw a blank version of Figure 12 and fill it in for yourself, paying particular interest to the inner and mid circles. In the outer circles, add those who come to mind first and have potential to move to the mid circle.

How strong does it look? Where do you need to add more names or move some up a level?

(*Note*: just like SAs, networking is about creating connections and mutually beneficial relationships. If you are always thinking about how you can add value to others, you'll stand out as a person worth being connected to.)

Website and search engine optimisation (SEO)
You'll notice the first three strategies revolve around personal relationships. The reason for that is simple – people buy from people. Consider this the foundation for your business. Of course, you may not be someone who thrives on building relationships with others. If that's you, find sales people who do.

There used to be a day when SEO was not relevant for some businesses due to the demographic they serve not being internet savvy, but those days are well on their way out; for most industries, they are gone. Sure, there are still small subsections of people who are not online, but I would feel very unsure suggesting it's okay not to look at SEO for any business.

(*Note*: if you're unsure what SEO is all about, essentially it's about having your website found on the internet by people who are looking for solutions to problems you solve.)

I'm not going to attempt to outline here what you need to do to optimise your SEO because, by the time I've written it, it will have changed. An internet search will bring up most of what you need to know and provide you with a good jumping-off point.

If SEO is really not in your wheelhouse of interest or expertise, outsource it. Just make sure you educate yourself enough before you do. As with all experts, there is a massive range of competency in this area.

If SEO is the art of being found on the internet, and the first step of your internet strategy, the second step is to have a website that can convert that initial interest into a lead or sale. How you do this will depend on your business and what problems you are solving. Things like price point, perceived risk of purchase and brand credibility will all influence the process.

The beautiful thing about internet marketing and website conversion is that it's so measurable. You will know very quickly what is working and what is not. Using Google Analytics and other tools, you can see pretty much everything. You can see how people are finding your site, how they are interacting with it, where they are dropping off, which pages are converting (meaning people are taking the actions you want them to; eg clicking a button or calling you) and how well. The list is almost endless. You can even track where peoples focus through their mouse movements.

The most important things are to know what you want people to do when they get to your site. What is your conversion strategy? Do you want them to call you, download something, sign up for something or buy at that moment? This will ensure the time and money invested in SEO will be optimised in terms of leads being generated.

Become an authority: publish, speak and get quoted

For some reason, those who publish, speak or are quoted in the media are given a higher platform of credibility to stand on. The public tends to perceive these people as better informed, having more skill or being more competent compared to someone in the same field who has not created the same exposure.

To some degree, I guess it makes sense. To publish, speak or be quoted takes a lot of work (trust me, I know), so that effort should have some reward.

Think about the problems your ideal clients have (remember back to your marketing blueprint) and what topic you could write about that will help them out. Also consider the best place be to be published (in the minds of your ideal customers).

No doubt you have heard the saying 'they've written the book on that' when someone is enquiring about a person's level of expertise in a particular area. That is said not because they have written the book on the subject but because they know enough to be able to.

The other beautiful thing about putting your expertise in writing is it forces you to get clear in your thinking. You need to be able to articulate yourself in a way the reader will understand. And it's not until you put pen to paper that you realise how scattered your thinking may be.

When you are crystal clear about your area of expertise, you will develop a new level of confidence, and your skill set will naturally rise. Whether you're a window manufacturer talking about what makes a quality window or a dry goods importer talking about the quality of ingredients, there is an area to write about.

It need not be a full-blown book. You can write blog articles published on your site and others (this helps your SEO), downloadable white papers (helps your conversion on your website) or newspaper columns (you'll most likely need to pay for this), or have a radio spot.

You might need to get a little creative to find your angle when speaking. An example is a client of ours who is in the meal preparation business. They talk to groups of busy mums about tips and tricks for being more organised and getting more time for themselves (ie, living a calmer life). This topic resonates with a lot of people and enables our client to weave in their service and share some customer success stories.

Again, it's back to what problems your ideal customers have, and how you can package a solution, either through speaking or writing, to address the issue and gain exposure for your business.

CONVERSION RATE

Measure

The simple act of measurement has amazing effects. We covered this earlier under the topic of measuring, so we won't repeat it here. The long and short is, if you do not measure your conversion rate, guaranteed you are leaving money on the table.

If you measure it and review it on a frequent basis, it will raise the awareness of you and your team, and will subsequently influence your actions.

Sales process

A sales process is the map of the steps required to move someone from an enquiry to a sale. The complexity of this process will vary depending on the size of the sale, the typical length of the sales cycle and the risk profile of the purchaser.

In short, your sales process should:
- build rapport
- build credibility
- reduce buying resistance
- increase buying acceptance
- understand the true needs of your prospect
- establish value in the mind of the buyer
- address the common and predictable objections
- make the experience feel comfortable for both parties
- bring the process to a natural close.

A good sales process is one that is somewhat scripted (meaning the sales person knows the key points to cover/ questions to ask; a good script means you don't sound like someone who is scripted).

Ideally, you would have your process set up in your CRM and be able to measure each stage for the length of time needed to move forwards, and conversion rate. When you have this kind of data, it allows for continuous refinement.

USP and guarantee

Knowing what makes you different and how that benefits your customers is a key point in sales. This can be done through a conversation, website copy, information package sent to prospects or whatever means is fitting for your sales process.

The important thing is knowing what your USP is and clearly communicating that to your prospects (as covered in the section 'Your marketing blueprint').

A fitting example my friend Mike, who I mentioned runs a renovation contracting business. Part of the business's positioning is its quality guarantee and the fact it is not the cheapest. When he communicates this to a prospect, he quickly gets a response that guides both him and the prospect as to whether this is going to be a good fit. If it is, he knows his time quoting the job is going to be well invested. It also prepares the prospect for a higher price, but an excellent quality project.

Guarantees can be extremely powerful. One of the key reasons people hesitate or fail to buy is because of the perceived risk they see in doing so. Most perceived risks are emotional. Knowing this gives you the ability to identify what emotion is driving the thought process of your prospect, and craft a guarantee that takes hesitation off the table.

Guarantees are generally around giving people peace of mind and reassurance that when they choose to spend, it's going to be a good decision. It lowers the risk in their mind.

Many businesses will do whatever it takes to keep a customer happy. Why not advertise that? Most people don't because they think if they do, people will take advantage of it and they will lose money. The reality is, maybe a small percentage will do that, but the clear majority will not, and the benefits you will reap from the guarantee – and its effect on your conversion rate – will greatly outweigh any small percentage of people who take advantage. Most people are good people – remember that.

For more information on this topic, refer to the section Your marketing blueprint.

Testimonials

It's questionable whether your prospects will believe what you say about yourself (eg 'We are always on time and will respond to you within twelve hours'), but they will believe past customers who share their experience. Written testimonials are good, but video testimonials are best.

Give your best customers a few questions to answer on video, then get a video editor to clip them together to form a powerful video testimonial. It's great if the video is high quality, but it's okay if it's not. It is better to shoot a testimonial on the spot using your smartphone than to miss the opportunity because the logistics of lining up a time with your videographer and client become too difficult.

Here are some prompting questions you can use.

1. What were the important considerations for you when looking for a _____ ?
2. What was it that led you to choose us? How are we different from other _____ ?

3. What concerns did you have about buying/hiring a
   _____ ?
4. What was your experience in dealing with us?
5. What would you say to others who are in a similar situation to you who are looking for a _____ ?

There are a few key ways to getting powerful testimonials.

- Make it easy. Even offer to write it yourself and have the customer approve it.
- Ask when the emotion is high and positive. This might sound obvious, but you really need to strike while the iron is hot.
- Get as much quantitative information as you can (ie measurable results). General comments like, 'They were really easy to deal with' and 'They were really nice' are okay, but if the customer can explicitly communicate the tangible benefits, that is more powerful. It is much better to have specific comments like, 'They delivered three days before they said they would and helped us to cut our costs by thirteen per cent.'
- Thank your customer once you receive the testimonial.

Sales speed and follow-up

The law of diminishing enthusiasm is real. All things being equal, the longer it takes for someone to buy, the less chance there is of them buying. Develop the ability to measure your sales speed (time between a prospect becoming a lead and them buying), and you'll soon see there is a tipping point, after which your conversion rate drops, sometimes dramatically so.

Of course, this is not to suggest that just pushing someone to make a sale sooner is going to result in a yes; it's more about your assertiveness in running your sales process.

When you can establish optimal time frames for each step in your sales process, your sales team's awareness and behaviour will change. Instead of waiting until tomorrow to make that follow-up call, the metrics say it needs to happen today, so there is more chance of the sale happening today.

This is the science side of sales. The data will guide you on best practices.

RETENTION
Show them the love
This is an overriding philosophy that should permeate all customer interactions and inform your mindset toward customer service.

People can sense how you feel about them. Have you ever had an experience as a customer where it all went wrong, however, you could tell the business was really trying, and cared about making it right?

In our experience, your intent and mindset toward customer service have an almost immeasurable impact on your customer retention.

Be wary of becoming jaded on this approach by a possible minority of customers who are just a pain. Let them go and focus on the majority. Remember 80/20.

For the majority, show them how much you care and value them. This can be done in many ways. Here are just a few:
- telling your customers how much you appreciate them
- sending thank you cards, ideally hand written

- articulating (and putting in writing) your beliefs and values around your customers and how they should be treated, and then training your team
- ensuring your team are on board with this mindset and show it in every interaction with customers.
- encourage your team by:
  - sharing positive feedback from customers with them
  - making a big deal when your team is showing the right behaviours in customer service
  - sharing examples or drawing analogies of experiences your team have had as the customer.

After-sale follow-up

If you think about most transactions you make with businesses, how often do you hear from that business after the sale has been made? You might perhaps receive an offer to buy more, but how often do you, for instance, receive a card thanking you for being a customer?

What would your customers think if they got one from you? Do you think it would make you stand out? Do you think it would communicate the message, 'we care about you'?

Making a sale should be the start of a relationship, not the end of the sales process. Find ways to reach out and check in to make sure everything you helped them with is still working out.

This act alone will generate referrals and repeat business.

Regular communication

Allow the same lines as follow-up, keep in touch with your

customers. One of the best ways to do this is through a newsletter. The trick to newsletters is making them valuable. The measure of value is how much they help the intended audience, including how well they are presented and easy to digest.

Craft your newsletter in a way that provides ongoing value. When someone gets your newsletter in their inbox, you want them to think, 'Oh good! I want to read that.' They may or may not depending on how busy they are, but the point is how well your newsletter is perceived.

What ideas can you share with your customers that will help them in their business or life? What relevant news might they be interested in? What customer stories can you share that might inspire or educate them?

Of course, it's okay to tie a little promotion with your communications. You want to make sure any promotion is tasteful and less than 15 per cent of the publication in terms of focus and space.

There will be times to break this rule, but in general, you should be doing a whole lot more giving than asking. When people feel you have given a lot, they don't mind you asking occasionally. When it's the other way around – well, you know how it feels.

Member's clubs and community

Everyone likes to feel special, and there is something about reward/membership/loyalty programs that can work well. Different formats will fit different businesses, but the overall goal is to make people feel special and a part of something. When someone feels included, it gives them a dopamine hit. It's a good feeling.

Perhaps there are perks, specials, invitation-only events, priority service and so on that make someone stick with your brand.

Membership and community are a strategy to layer on top of an excellent product or service. They are not a replacement for excellence. Just ask most US-based airlines.

If you can deliver in a way that gives your customers the wow feeling, it shows them how much you care about them and makes them feel special by being part of a community or membership. There are only a handful of reasons why you'll lose that customer. And it will rarely be because of the price.

Evolve the customer experience

Occasionally, staying the same is a necessary strategy, but not often. People change, the market changes and your business needs to change as a result. Be mindful of trends and patterns and stay a step ahead, or at least on pace.

Make your website more user-friendly and interactive as the technology allows you to. Use automated reminders to make your customer's life easier. Deliver content specific to their interests rather than blanketing everyone with the same message. These are just a few examples of what is possible today that was not possible 10, or even 5, years ago.

A company that does not evolve the customer experience as technology and trends progress will eventually lose customers to those that do. Goodwill and caring will get you so far, but if you are not evolving the way you work with your customers, you are possibly making it harder for them, which is the opposite of caring. We live in a more convenient and customised world, and it's only going to get more so. Be sure to keep up – better still, be the leader.

CUSTOMER SPEND

Eliminate discounting

The biggest killer of profitability is the default use of discounting to win business. If you need to discount, it's usually a sign of one (or all) of the following:

1. weak or no USP (see the Conversion rate section), or you aren't doing a good job of communicating it
2. poor sales process or sales skills
3. your marketing is bringing in the wrong type of prospects (revisit the Your marketing blueprint section).
4. sabotaging beliefs about you and your company's value.

Case study: Framing shop

When we helped Julie (owner of a framing and design shop) calculate the costs of her discounting practices and looked at the reasons she was discounting, it became clear it was largely being done through habit and a feeling she had to.

We challenged Julie to reduce discounting and she attacked it with vigour. Through increased awareness (what gets measured gets managed), some better options (adding value versus discounting) and a clearer USP, she almost eliminated the discounting culture with no loss in conversion. And it all flowed directly to the bottom line.

Pricing

In the same class as discounting, having prices too low makes being profitable hard. Most of the fear of increasing prices lies with the sales people and business owner. Ask yourself what level of value you would need to feel confident you are delivering to justify a 10 per cent price increase.

Case study: Print and quick copy

When I asked Sam (owner of a quick print shop) about why he had not increased prices in 3 years, his response was, 'Our customers are too price sensitive.' I asked, 'Do you mind if we test that assumption?' He was open to a test, so for each quote that came in over the next 2 weeks, we applied a 10 per cent price increase. The result was 10 per cent more profit, and almost no pushback. Be wary of your assumptions – they affect the way people respond.

While I'm not advocating everyone out there should do an across-the-board price increase, chances are that for many people reading this book, it might just be what you should do.

Be clear about the value you provide, have a compelling USP and charge accordingly. Positioning yourself as premium and high quality is a valid differentiator. Price communicates quality.

Case study: Hair salon

Nicole and Simone had been running their salon for 6 years. They made 3 price increases within the first year of working with us. The first time they did it (with massive amounts of fear), a couple of customers did comment. They said, 'You've been too cheap for too long.' After the third price increase they did start to meet some resistance, but only from the more price-sensitive customers.

The customers you lose through pricing are, by and

large, more than compensated for by the extra profit you make from those who stay.

For a more detailed and statistical view on this, download our Increase versus discount pricing charts. There, you can see how much your total sales are able to drop before your profit is affected, based on your current margin and how much you want to increase your prices. jumpingoffthewheel.com

In most cases, you can be working a whole lot less (lower sales volume) and making more by tweaking your pricing. And if you do lose customers due to a price increase, which customers do you think you'll lose? Yep … most often the ones that we call PITAs (pains in the ass).

For example, if your current gross margin is 30 per cent and you discount by 10 per cent, you need to make 50 per cent more sales just to make the same amount of profit. But, if your current gross margin is 30 per cent and you increase prices by 10 per cent, you can lose 25 per cent of your sales and still make the same amount of profit.

Case study: Data storage and handling

When we started working with Bill, he confided it had been 7 years since he had increased prices. Bill had a good business but was leaving money on the table. After consulting with his team, they came up with an increase that for some long-term customers was going to be close to a 50 per cent increase. We looked at the possible outcomes of the increase and it all made sense to proceed.

The notices went out, and out of 500-odd customers, there were less than 30 enquiries/comments. Of those, only a handful needed massaging and some special attention to keep on board.

Before the increase, Bill's business turned over around $4.6 million annually and its net profit margin was around 8 per cent (not great). After the increase, when all the dust settled, the net margin was up to 26 per cent.

I'm not suggesting everyone can make an increase like Bill. However, the lesson to take from Bill is that for 7 years he and his team stood still on pricing. What could their business have looked like if they had addressed the mental block on pricing earlier? What is your mental block on pricing?

Value add/upsell

When Julie at the framing store made customers aware of the benefits of clear glass in their framing job, more customers were saying yes, resulting in 5 per cent added value to the sale, and a better product for the customer.

We see these opportunities in sales situations all the time. It's the classic 'Would you like fries with that?' approach that McDonald's made so famous.

Think about gross profit dollars generated per sale. Sometimes it's worth sacrificing margin percentage to increase margin dollars. Retailers do this prolifically and for a good reason. And there's no reason other industries can't do it as well.

Here's an example of how it works:
- sale (A) value $200 at 50 per cent margin = $100 gross profit
- sale (B) value $300 at 40 per cent margin = $120 gross profit

This type of strategy makes sense if there is little chance the customer of sale (A) would have later returned to buy what was sold in sale (B)'s upsell.

In my family business (printing), I was schooled in the upsell. We would ask customers if they would like a UV varnish on their job (a UV varnish really makes a print job look stunning) or have it die cut rather than square cut (more premium finish), better papers and so on. These suggestions made for a better product; that is, they added true value for our customer. Customers didn't always say yes, but the percentage that did made a significant impact on the bottom line.

The lesson here is: if you don't ask, you don't get. And often your customers are not aware of the options available to them that can give them more value.

Email marketing

Staying engaged with your customers, keeping them informed and bringing them opportunities to buy are all critical to customer spend and retention rate, but the way you do this will vary according to your industry and the relationship you have with your customers.

A commercial diving client of ours sends out a quarterly newsletter to its clients and prospects profiling the jobs it has done recently. It also interviews a team member and shares some stories about them (people love stories). This supplements the phone calls the business makes to customers mining for more work. It gives a conversation opener: 'Hey, did you see the job we did at … I thought of you guys and ….'

At SalesUp! we send out a high-value education publication to our stakeholders twice a month (*Business*

Nutrition – go to salesup.com.au/business-nutrition to subscribe) that contains the latest thinking, trends, tools and interviews with business legends to help people in their business. We include a subtle promotion every so often giving our readers the chance to buy from us.

With today's technology, you can tailor the content and offers you send to your customers and prospects. When people get timely offers that are of interest to them, from people they trust, there is a high probability they will buy.

What else do they need?
There are usually two reasons why we don't sell more to our existing customers.
1. We assume they know what we have to offer and believe they don't want it.
2. We just don't think about it. We are too focused on finding new customers.

I was always surprised when I worked in our family business to discover customers who would come in for a press check (to make sure we had the job right before doing a big print run) and would look around our reception-area product displays and say, 'I didn't know you guys did …'

Just like many businesses I see, we fell into the trap of myopic thinking and not educating our customers on all we can do for them.

Case study: Financial planning

Peter, owner-operator of a financial planning company, spe-
cialises in insurance for business owners. His marketing plan
for a 6-month period came from the following exercise.

He drew up a matrix listing his top 20 per cent of customers down one side and his product offerings across the
top. He then cross-referenced and checked off who had
which products. He then went through a second time and,
knowing what he did about his customers, highlighted
which products certain customers should have, given their
stage of life.

He found many gaps and subsequently started educating his customers about where they might be exposed.
From this exercise, I also ended up with a couple of new
policies myself (which, of course, I did need).

Even if you believe you are selling all you can to your
customers, think about what else they may need that you
don't currently sell. It's likely there is still more that they
need. What else could you be selling them? Add to your
range where it makes sense or refer to an alliance partner,
and set up up a commission arrangement. When you think
about it that way, the options are endless.

GROSS MARGIN

A couple of the fastest ways to increase your margins have
been covered already in terms of eliminating discounting
and pricing. Knowing they hit 2 of the 6 drivers makes them
very powerful strategies. Here are some others on our go-to
list.

Cost accounting

It's very hard to make a process or product more efficient if you don't know what it costs you to produce. And when you do have access to dependable data, you can share it with those who can affect it.

Accurately measuring labour and materials back to specific jobs can sometimes be a tricky thing depending on your business, but with today's technology and software, it's easier than ever.

Know your true costs. The increased awareness alone will yield results.

Efficiency

To improve the profitability of a product or service, you either charge more for it or reduce costs internally to make it cheaper to produce. Pricing covers the first part, and efficiency can be a large component of the second.

The Cost accounting section covered getting the data. This strategy is all about improving it.

Get your team involved in developing some goals and targets you think are achievable. Map out the actions with a who-does-what-by-when, along with the appropriate measure to know if you are on track.

Case study: My family business – printing

Early in my career, when I was an assistant production manager in our family business, one of my early mentors, Rod, would continually remind me of a powerful lesson whenever I was tempted to take shortcuts to expedite a rush job. He would say, 'Jamie, the long way is the short way.'

In other words, the chances of error if you take the shortcut are way higher, and you'll just end up doing the job over and taking longer than if you had just done it right the first time. Or, as the carpenter says, 'Measure twice, cut once.'

Measure your error rates and develop a culture of getting it right the first time.

Targets and sharing information (open-book management)

Old-school thinking is to keep financial information close to your chest for fear that if everyone knew the financials … well, I can't imagine.

We all have our reasons, and this strategy is not for everyone. However, I do know that when people are well educated in how to read the numbers, and they can see the benefit to them from improving them (profit sharing), people feel trusted and engaged. It's very hard for a person to feel genuinely trusted if you withhold information from them. Despite all other aspects of the relationship, at a subconscious level, non-sharing sabotages trust.

I used the phrase above 'educated in how to read the numbers', as this is a critical component in sharing information. If the information is shared without context or education, it can have a damaging effect.

In a company that does not share financial information, it's very common for employees to think the company (and owners) make way more money than is the reality. And at some level, they may think that any attempt to become more efficient or grow will just be a way to line the owners' pockets with more cash. Open-book management and profit sharing is a way of aligning interests, and it must be done with an intentional approach with a proven methodology.

To outline a methodology and implementation guide about open-book management is outside the scope of this book, and truthfully, there are already some great ones out there. For my recommendations, download our recommended reading list from the resource section – jumpingoffthewheel.com.

On our blog, there is also a great interview with Norm Jefferies on how he implemented open-book management. He covers the good, the bad and the interesting. You can find the interview at salesup.com.au/business_nutrition/vol-10/.

Enrol your team in target development, action plans and rhythm of execution. Employees are way more competent than most people give them credit for.

Your people have ideas and the potential to improve radically the operational efficiency of your company. Tap into that.

Technology
Software today can be a game changer. The right software will give you access to data that will help you make better decisions, and it will also make you more efficient. It will simplify communications, reduce time spent looking for information, give you real-time data and increase response rates to customer questions. Faster quotes lead to improved conversions, retention and happier customers. Speed can affect customer spend as they want to buy more from you because it's easy, and it leads people to refer more because of your fast service.

Look closely where your team is spending the most time – this could be an area to optimise through technology.

Case study: Manufacturing

A manufacturing client of ours upgraded its accounting system to be cloud based and implemented a scanning system to streamline its paperwork. Work that used to take five people in the office all their time to do is now done easily by three. All this while growing at 100 per cent per year.

The business's next steps are new enterprise management systems that will link in with its accounting software and give it real-time information for project management and accurate departmental profitability. We love that!

Focus on higher-margin products and services

Once you know your true margins across all products and services, you can better focus on those with a higher margin. Be sure to look at true margins (allowing for overhead required for each product or service) and account for things like freight, which are often overlooked.

Case study: Commercial diving

Our commercial diving client could make huge margins on sewer treatment plant projects (ewww). But it turns out, it was bridge inspections that gave the client higher profitability. This was based on equipment needs, overhead and admin requirements, and chance of mistakes. When the business analysed past jobs, this all became clear, yet before looking closely at the numbers, it assumed sewers were the better jobs to do because of the much higher day rates and overall sales numbers.

The business then refocused and developed its USP and

marketing efforts around bridges – sales took off. More importantly, profits exploded.

OVERHEAD
Budgets and review spending
A very simple, yet commonly overlooked, strategy is to review what you are spending money on. As mentioned, there are only two reasons to spend money on business:
1. to get customers
2. to keep customers.

Chances are very good that you're spending money right now on things that contribute nothing to either of these reasons. It can be a great temptation (particularly in good times) to pimp your ride and get extravagant in spending. Some personalities are more at risk of this than others.

When you develop an overhead budget (think back to your profit model and making profit non-negotiable) and you can accurately report on it each month, you'll have a keener eye on where you choose to spend money.

Reduce spending now with the goal of overhead/sales down every year
In line with the previous section, challenge everyone who spends money in your company to reduce it by 1 per cent of sales every quarter for four quarters in a row.

For example, if your overhead is currently $120,000 per quarter and sales are $300,000 per quarter, you have an overhead ratio of 40 per cent. Your challenge would be to reduce it to 39 per cent in the first quarter, 38 per cent in second quarter and so on to end up with a 36 per cent ratio by the end of the year. If your sales stayed at the same level, that would be an extra $48,000 of profit each year moving forward.

Make it a competition with rewards each quarter. It does not need to be monetary – a gimmicky award can often do the trick. Make it fun! If you have profit sharing in place, there is also the natural reward built in to align with the behaviour you want.

Another powerful way to view spending is to understand how much in sales is required to cover the expense you are about to incur. If you were about to put a new TV into your boardroom, think about how much you need to sell to recover the cost.

Case study: Waterproofing

When Rick, owner of a waterproofing company did this, it made him see his expenses in a different light and he quickly put a red pen through many expenses he'd previously been able to justify through some biased logic.

Accountability for spending

When someone's name is next to each line item on the P&L, and they need to justify it to the team in your financial review each month (because you have or are going to have one of these … right?), it's amazing how it can alter behaviour, particularly if you have profit sharing in place. Who wants to be the person who is eating into the profits?

Negotiate everything

Everything is negotiable. You always want to be fair to your suppliers and look for a win/win relationship, but that does not mean you need to pay more than you should.

If you can't negotiate a better price for a product or service, negotiate a discount based on payment terms (eg if you pay within 30 days, you get a 2 per cent discount). Play around with this concept because many companies value cash flow more than profit. If you've got strong cash flow (refer to the Maximising and managing cash flow section), you can afford to pay faster and take advantage of discounts.

The same can apply to bulk purchasing, which is not great for cash flow, but again, if you've done your homework there, it gives you the ability to consider this option. Or join a buying group so you can get bulk prices without having to take all the excess stock yourself.

Outsourcing
In today's world, this is easier than ever. The ability to outsource means that tasks that are not within your company's competency or that you don't have enough volume to justify hiring for can easily be taken care of without incurring the fixed cost of an employee.

Common and easily outsourced tasks are things like admin, marketing, sales assistance (follow-up and database management) and IT. Even hiring a virtual CFO is a great option rather than hiring someone in-house. You can often get access to higher-level expertise through outsourcing than you can afford to hire for in-house. It's kind of like renting versus owning your own home, particularly in an expensive city. Your dollars go much further renting with respect to what you get for your money.

With the explosion of outsourcing companies and

crowd-sourced websites, you now have unbelievable access to a massively wide range of expertise for a fraction of what it would cost you to hire internally.

That is not to suggest that this strategy is foolproof. In fact, you'll probably need to be more diligent in your selection and operational processes to make outsourcing work smoothly. There are plenty of stories of outsourcing going wrong. So, proceed with caution.

That said, with the right outsource partners, it's a very viable strategy.

PLANNING

An important ingredient to successful execution is a clear plan that lays out *who* needs to do *what* by *when*. After reading the preceding material, you may be tempted with lots of ideas to get out there and start doing! While getting out there and making it happen is noble, it's way better to do some thinking and planning around it first.

In our model, there are two major components of your written plan and one optional component depending on your company set-up.

The major components are:
- a 90-day plan: overview of top 1 to 5 priorities for the quarter (*who* does *what* by *when*)
- a marketing activity calendar: details on specific marketing activity levels.

The optional component is:
- a one-page sales plan – for companies with sales people.

(*Note*: no business plans here. Business plans have their place: when you are starting out and need to get clear on the lie of the land, or when you are going for financing – a business plan gives financiers peace of mind that you know what you're doing – but in my opinion, they have little use in day-to-day execution. They usually just sit on the shelf and collect dust. What we are after is a plan you can act on.

A 90-day plan

A 90-day plan is your tool to stay focused. Running a business can pull you in many different directions, and without something to keep you grounded and on track, it can be easy to find yourself spinning your wheels and not gaining meaningful traction.

Have you ever walked into your office on a Monday morning and thought, 'Where do I start?' Having a well-thought-out 90-day plan helps answer that question.

WHY 90 DAYS?

Our minds can have a tough time switching from long-term thinking to short-term thinking in the heat of the moment. And because day-to-day operations are mostly short-term thinking, it can be difficult to consider long-term goals while you're trying to conduct day-to-day business.

So, 90 days is a time frame that is long enough to get meaningful things done, but not so long that it feels way off down the track. It's a time frame that provides the right level of urgency and pressure, yet gives scope to tackle important projects.

To create a meaningful and strategically fitting 90-day plan, you must consider the long-term goals of your business. To solely focus on the next 90 days, while better than no plan at all, can often leave you switching directions every 90-days because you have no context to decide which way to go.

For that reason, we guide our clients through a process, starting from 3 to 5 years out, getting clear on the longer-term goals they have for the business. Once this picture has been created, we are able to set some 1-year milestone goals that, if achieved, will have them on course for the longer-term goals.

The 1-year goals can (and should) be very specific. We use the time-tested SMART philosophy for goal setting: Specific, Measurable, Achievable, Results-oriented with a Time frame. This ensures the goals are well thought out, and the client is clear on recognising when they've achieved the goal. They know what success looks like.

Goals that don't follow the SMART philosophy tend to be the fluffy or abstract type of goals and have several problems.

- They are hard to communicate to others.
- It's hard to know how much effort to put in to achieve them. For example, if your goal was simply to grow sales, how much effort do you put behind that? Compare that to a goal such as grow sales by 20 per cent. Now the level of activity required to make that happen becomes a lot clearer.
- It's not very inspiring. When something is foggy (ie you are not clear), you simply can't commit to it, and the level of engagement and action that flows from it will be lacking (refer to the First Principles: See your vision and Planning brings clarity).

SMART goals put pressure on all involved because they are measurable. There is no hiding or bluffing your way forwards. Either you're on track, or you're not.

CREATING A 90-DAY PLAN

As just mentioned, we've developed a process for creating a well-thought-out, actionable 90-day plan. You can download it from the resource section of this book's website (jumpingoffthewheel.com). It has five major steps.

1. *Long-term goals.* Have a good idea of the direction you are heading and what it looks like. Think 3 to 5 years at least. Thinking even longer is a good idea if you can. Personally, I like to think in 10-year chunks for this exercise. The strength, clarity and importance of your vision will directly correlate with the power of your plans and actions (refer to First Principle, See your vision).

2. *One-year goals.* Look at your 3, 5 or 10-year vision and boil it down to some 1-year goals that, when achieved, will put you on track. Concrete SMART.

3. *Financials.* Now we need to put some numbers to it. Look at your historical numbers and then forecast your financials (mainly your P&L; including your balance sheet is great if you are able) relative to your 1-year goals.

4. *90-day priorities.* What are the 1 to 5 (less is more here – it's okay to have just 1) strategies that must be done this quarter to be on track for your 1-year goals. Examples of strategies were outlined previously under The 20 per cent growth strategies (our top 5).

5. *Strategy details.* Once you've identified the 1 to 5 strategies, it's important to flush out all the detail (ie who does what by when). It's also a good idea to map out any costs

associated, plus the amount of time that will be required to get it done. This often helps make sure the plan is realistic. (*Note*: a common trap is loading too much on your plan. Taking a critical look at the estimated time required often helps temper unrealistic workloads. For example, let's say that one of your strategies is to develop a strategic partnership with Acme Co. You would list out all the steps you need to take to make that happen, who should do it, as well as time and cost estimates.)

ONE-PAGE SUMMARY

At the end of this process, your goal is to have a plan that fits onto one page. That page should show:

- 1-year goals
- 90-day strategies
- strategy task details with associated timelines.

Figure 13 shows a sample of a one-page 90-day plan from our 90-day planning tool.

CRITICAL ACTIVITIES AND CRITICAL INDICATORS

Your 90-day plan gives a good overview of the top 1 to 5 priorities for the quarter, and these are the proactive strategies that will move you toward your longer-term goals. They may or may not be sales and marketing related.

On top of these 1 to 5 priorities are the everyday critical sales and marketing activities that must be executed consistently to drive your growth targets. The planning of these is detailed in the Marketing activity calendar section. First, let's understand a couple of key terms – critical activities and critical indicators.

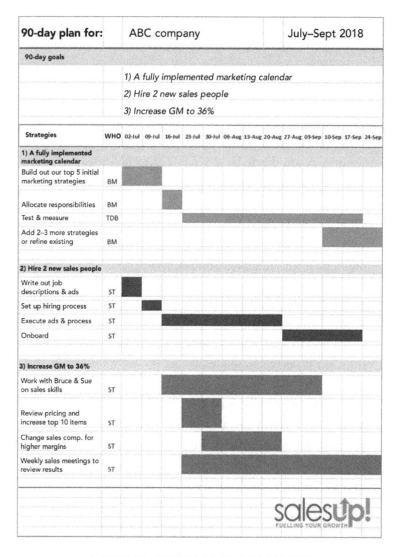

90-day plan for:	ABC company	July–Sept 2018

90-day goals

1) A fully implemented marketing calendar
2) Hire 2 new sales people
3) Increase GM to 36%

Strategies	WHO	02-Jul	09-Jul	16-Jul	23-Jul	30-Jul	06-Aug	13-Aug	20-Aug	27-Aug	03-Sep	10-Sep	17-Sep	24-Sep
1) A fully implemented marketing calendar														
Build out our top 5 initial marketing strategies	BM													
Allocate responsibilities	BM													
Test & measure	TDB													
Add 2–3 more strategies or refine existing	BM													
2) Hire 2 new sales people														
Write out job descriptions & ads	ST													
Set up hiring process	ST													
Execute ads & process	ST													
Onboard	ST													
3) Increase GM to 36%														
Work with Bruce & Sue on sales skills	ST													
Review pricing and increase top 10 items	ST													
Change sales comp. for higher margins	ST													
Weekly sales meetings to review results	ST													

salesup!
FUELLING YOUR GROWTH

FIGURE 13: ONE-PAGE 90-DAY SAMPLE

Visit the resource section of the website to download a copy of these templates plus the associated workbook that will guide you through the process.
jumpingoffthewheel.com

Critical activities

Critical activities are the tasks that you and your team have direct control over, and that influence sales results. They are sales and marketing activities that are 100 per cent within your control, and can either generate an opportunity for a sale or convert an opportunity to a sale.

An example of a critical activity would be an email marketing campaign or phone calls to prospective or repeat customers.

Critical indicators

Critical indicators are the measurements and numbers that help you to see if your critical activities are being effective. These numbers will allow you to predict sales and cash flow.

An example of a critical indicator might be a certain number of quotes. You can't directly affect how many quotes come in; however, measuring the volume might tell you if your marketing strategies such as email campaigns, which are a critical activity, have been effective. In this example, measuring your number of quotes and combining it with your conversion rate (what percentage of quotes you win on average) allows you to forecast your sales volume.

> **Critical activities** are the 'What are we doing to grow?'
> **Critical indicators** are the 'How well are we doing it?'

What we want to know is: which activities, if done consistently and skilfully at the right magnitude, will ensure the most predictable flow of sales?

As you move through the exercise of working out your critical activities and critical indicators, you might run into some grey areas. These are things you are not sure are activities or are indicators. The way to determine if something is a critical activity is how much control you have over it.

A good example of a grey area is the number of prospect meetings. You could argue that meetings are not 100 per cent within your control because, first, someone needs to agree to have the meeting (outside of your control – mostly) and they must keep the appointment (outside your control – mostly). However, it's also fair to say that if you have an effective methodology of attaining meetings and you do enough activity, you will get meetings. So, in this case, I would argue it's enough within your sphere of influence to call it a critical activity. At the end of the day, it's your call to determine what feels right for your business.

If you are unsure if an activity is worthy of being a critical activity, try using it for a while, and after a period, review the results. If you can link a person's activity to results, it's probably okay to use it as a critical activity.

Case study: Legal practice

We knew from some earlier measuring efforts that a key source of referrals for our client Susan was her banking and accounting partners. We could also see that there was a lot more potential to be had from nurturing existing relationships than creating new ones. Susan felt the way to do this (given her style and love of food) was lunches with these contacts. So, number of lunches became her critical activity. (Who said critical activities had to be boring?) Her critical indicator was number of referrals from referral partners. Both are simple to measure and for her, turned out to be very effective.

For our business, one of our critical activities is speaking engagements. We know that when I present, in the audience will be several people who will want to speak to me about working with them. And from those discussions, several opportunities will arise. From the resulting opportunities, a certain percentage will be a good fit, and we'll work together.

So, for us, the critical activity is the number of speaking engagements. Our critical indicator is the number of opportunities generated. The first is in our control. The second tells us how effective our critical activity is. If we were generating lots of speaking engagements, but no opportunities were flowing from them, it would be no use patting ourselves on the back for generating lots of speaking engagements. Clearly, something would need to change.

Your critical indicators may be something you add to your dashboard, as covered in the Data and reporting section. Or, they may be tracked on individual dashboards for sales people (see the One-page sales plan section).

Marketing activity calendar
A marketing activity calendar is simply a way of planning out the critical activities you've identified. It allows you to see the magnitude of activity and who should do what by when.

There may be times, particularly if you've got sales people, when you will need a one-page sales plan in addition to the marketing activity calendar. You'll know as you get into it, the format that will work best for you and your team.

sales up!
FUELLING YOUR GROWTH

Marketing Calendar	Mth1 Jan			Mth2 Feb			Mth3 Mar		
	Who	#	$	Who	#	$	Who	#	$
INTERNAL VEHICLES									
Check out POS for upsell									
Uniforms	TR		30	TR		50	TR		50
Curb signage			50						
Invoice stuffers									
Referral competition							TR		1000
ONLINE VEHICLES									
Google Ad Words	JS		500	JS		500	JS		500
Blog post	JS	2		JS	2		JS	2	
Facebook ads	JS		100	JS		100	JS		100
LinkedIn article	JS	2		JS	2		JS	2	
YouTube video	JS	4		JS	4		JS	4	
TRADITIONAL VEHICLES									
Direct mail				SG	350	1000			
Magazine ad	SG		500				SG		500
Speaking engagements									
Strategic alliances	SG	3	100	SG	3	100	SG	3	100
			$1,280			$1,750			$2,250
$14,030									

FIGURE 14: MARKETING ACTIVITY CALENDAR

This document should be as simple as possible. Simplicity allows for easy understanding and clear execution by all those involved. That said, simplicity should not replace thoroughness in thinking and planning. The three components of a marketing activity calendar are:

1. *What* are the critical activities you plan to use for new and existing customers?
2. *When* is it all going to happen?
3. *Who* is the champion? This may not necessarily be the person who does the work, but is the person accountable for its execution?

Ideally, you would have this set up to cover the next 6 months and review every quarter, at which point you roll forwards another 3 months. So, you've essentially got a rolling 6-month marketing activity calendar.

Figure 14 is a sample of what that might look like.

One-page sales plan

We are diving a little into sales management here, but the concept is important whether you've got one or 20 sales people. And please don't think you don't have any. If you think this, then *you* are the sales person.

The one-page sales plan is like the marketing activity calendar with a slight spin. I find that for most sales people, the activity levels can be set based on what a typical week should look like rather than how the activity will be rolled out over the quarter (as in the marketing activity calendar). The goal is to build some metrics around target sales activities per week. A one-page sales plan is also something that is unique and personal to the individual whereas a marketing activity calendar is usually an overall company document. Some of the things that might be included in a one-page sales plan are:

- number of existing customer visits/calls per week
- number of prospect visits/calls per week
- number of networking events
- number of strategic partner meetings.

The actual activity level of each week may vary from the targets set out, but it serves as a red flag if you or your sales team are consistently way off the numbers.

Equally important (and almost more important) is tracking and reporting these numbers and the associated critical indicators (eg number of quotes, conversion rates). Having this level of transparency helps to guide behaviour and problem solving.

The two core reasons why sales people don't hit their numbers are:

1. low activity levels (eg not making enough calls)
2. low quality of those activities (eg they are making lots of calls but just don't have the skills to be effective, or are calling the wrong people).

Without tracking the critical activities and critical indicators, it's impossible to know how to help them. The numbers are essential for diagnosing where the problem lies.

There could be a variety of reasons why either of the above points are not being achieved – that's where it becomes your job as the sales coach to ask quality questions to get to the bottom of the issue.

A one-page sales plan has five components.

1. The numbers:
   a. sales targets
   b. BAU (business as usual) forecast. This refers to the level of sales that could be expected if no proactive actions were taken (ie regular incoming orders and repeat business)
   c. the gap – sales targets minus BAU.
2. Key accounts: top 20 per cent of customers and what nurturing or opportunities exist within this group.
3. Key prospects: who they are and what actions need to be taken to turn them into customers.
4. Other business development strategies: a list of additional critical activities that may be necessary to generate the sales required to bridge the gap. (*Note*: it's very important to understand sales cycles. If there is a large gap to be made for the current quarter and your business has a long sales cycle, the gap may not be achievable this quarter. In that case, you'd better be planning now for next quarter. The time frame of your one-page sales plan needs to match your sales cycle.)
5. Professional development: how the sales person will improve this quarter.

For a complete template and guide for the 'one-page sales plan', see our resources section.
jumpingoffthewheel.com

A final note on planning

As with all concepts and strategies in this book, implementing them is a journey and can take time. If you apply one small piece at a time, master it, then move on to the next piece, you'll be successful in the long run. Don't feel pressured to have these planning tools implemented immediately and perfectly.

The level you are at will dictate the speed at which you can implement changes and improvements. Planning is a skill set. If you've never planned before, be okay with your first plan being a disaster. Rest assured, the next quarter will be better. And so on. Just keep at it. Once you've got the concepts, change the format or structure to better suit your style and your business, if necessary.

EXECUTION AND RHYTHM

So, you've got your numbers mapped out (profit model and 6-point growth model), you've analysed them and built a plan for growth (90-day plan + marketing activity calendar + one-page sales plan). That is all fantastic stuff, and extremely valuable, *but* if you and your team can't execute it, then it really isn't worth that much, is it?

They say an average plan executed well is far more valuable than the perfect plan executed poorly.

Be very aware of the planning coma. Or paralysis from analysis. Too much navel gazing and idealising can be crippling. At the end of the day, you and your team need to *do* something.

With that said, let's look at the essential elements that

execute: standards and accountability; visibility; meeting rhythm; and implementing a meeting rhythm.

Standards and accountability

By far the biggest influence on execution is your leadership and the culture you create. Through your leadership and culture (see the Playing rules section) you set the standards by which people will determine what is acceptable and what is not.

So, the starting point here is knowing what those standards are, then communicating them clearly and holding people accountable to those standards. When there is no accountability, it sends a non-verbal instruction that it's okay not to get something done.

Let's say, for instance, that you agree to start your weekly meeting at 8 am. If people drift in at 8:03, 8:05, 8:10 and nothing is said, what message you are sending? You don't need to make a scene of it, but you might pull those people aside after and have a quick word about it. To set the tone, at the end of the meeting you might ask the 'offenders' to stay back and have a word. The rest of the team will know what is going on.

If this style is a little out of your comfort zone (and for many it is), I would highly recommend the book *Crucial Conversations* by Kerry Patterson, Joseph Grenny, Ron Mc-Millan and Al Switzler. The authors outline a methodology for having tough or potentially uncomfortable conversations.

Also think back to our First Principle of the Respect Matrix. You are always looking for a win/win. When anyone on the team chooses to not live up to the standards, where are they choosing to play on The Respect Matrix?

Visibility

Your priorities as outlined in your plan should be in everyone's face. A plan on the shelf or stored deep in your hard drive will have little chance compared to the one that is on a whiteboard in the room where you have your weekly and daily meetings (we'll get to your meeting rhythm next).

What we see in our immediate physical environment affects our thinking. When you can see your plan, it brings an action to the forefront. Get it out in the open where everyone can see it.

Meeting rhythm

Put aside any preconceived ideas about meetings. Yes, I agree, they can be a waste of time if they are not structured correctly. But that is not what we're talking about here. We're talking about a critical tool that enables you and your team to stay on focus and maintain a rhythm that builds momentum.

Here's an outline that, when running properly, keeps the mojo flowing. Treat this meeting schedule as a template and adapt or change it as makes sense for your business.

DAILY – DEPARTMENTAL HUDDLES

This is a short 5- to 10-minute standing meeting that covers three things:

- biggest win from yesterday
- your number 1 priority for the day ahead
- asks, where are you stuck?

Each person has a chance to speak (keep it short and have a timekeeper if necessary). Anything that requires more discussion should be taken offline after the meeting. The purpose is to get people grounded, connected and focused on the day ahead.

WEEKLY – MANAGEMENT OPERATIONAL MEETING

For department heads and key management personnel. The meeting covers things like:

- work in progress
- client issues
- job timelines
- staffing (short term and tactical – not strategic; eg you might talk about needing a new receptionist to cover maternity leave, but you wouldn't talk about bringing on a marketing manager when you've never had one before)
  - equipment maintenance
  - vendor issues.

This meeting is basically for things that affect day-to-day operations that need to happen in the next 1 to 13 weeks. Bigger issues should be deferred to the monthly strategy meeting.

MONTHLY – STRATEGY MEETING

This meeting is for reviewing your strategic 90-day plan. Issues that will be covered here include:

- marketing initiatives
- capital and equipment needs
- key personnel issues (performance, compensation, succession, need for hiring etc)

- financial review:
  - last month's performance
  - review of dashboard, trends and KPIs
  - cash flow forecast
  - 90-day plan review.

Depending on the size and complexity of your business, you may break these topics into a couple of meetings (eg the Four Keys – money, growth, operations, and people). Or you may group these together in various combinations. The goal is to have as few meetings as possible, and to have the right people in the right meetings. Your controller or CFO might be wasting their time in the marketing meeting … but maybe not. You will know the best answer to this.

QUARTERLY
This will replace your monthly meeting once every quarter, and it's all about creating the next 90-day plan. See previous chapter 'Planning'. This should ideally be offsite and last approximately half a day. You may need longer when you first get going.

ANNUAL
This is a review of the past year and setting the priorities for the year ahead. You'll take some time to look at the 3- to 5-year goals and ensure they are still relevant. This planning session will form the backbone of each 90-day plan for the next 12 months. This should be offsite and will last 1 to 2 days.

Implementing a meeting rhythm

This entire process can look daunting. If meetings have not been your strong point to date, the place I would recommend starting with is either the daily huddle or the quarterly 90-day planning.

The daily huddle is a simple step, can be done without the backing of a larger plan and will start the meeting habit. It gives a rhythm and flow without complicating things. Once you are doing it, and see the benefit, move on to the 90-day planning.

The reason you may want to start with the 90-day planning is it gives direction but is not a massive commitment to planning and meetings. It will force you to set the time aside and consider some questions you may not have asked before.

If you start with the 90-day planning, it's a good idea to piggy-back the daily huddle with this as your way of maintaining momentum.

OPERATIONS

THE WORD OPERATIONS is probably self-explanatory to you, and it's where most business owners feel at home. It's the day-to-day operating of the business in terms of making or delivering the product or service for your customer.

This part of the Four Keys framework is all about efficiency and how to scale without blowing yourself up.

Everyone can grow a business to a certain point through hard work, but then it can get to the point when there is just too much to keep up with, mistakes start happening, and the growth can feel out of control. It's when you are running at full pace on the hamster wheel without an end in sight that it can become obvious a better way is needed.

This section outlines the better way. And as with the previous two keys, there are four components to the Operations Key:

1. time choices
2. roles and responsibilities
3. workflow maps and systems

4. technology.

Let's take a look.

TIME CHOICES

The way you and your team use time is a key skill that drives your business success. If you are ineffective with how you use time, then all the knowledge, strategies and tactics in the world won't make any difference because you'll never have the time to implement them.

Note the heading of this section is Time choices. Referring back to our First Principle of Radical responsibility, it's easy to use lack of time as an excuse. The reality is, it's our choice how we use time, not time itself that is the problem. Lack of time is never a valid excuse.

My goal here is not to convince you how important it is to be intentional with your time choices because I'm assuming you buy into that already. My goal here is to recognise the pitfalls that compromise effectiveness and boost ownership of our time choices.

Important distinction: time choices is not about getting more done. It's about getting the right things done. That is the difference between efficiency and effectiveness. Be a person who values effectiveness over efficiency. And yes, having both is optimal.

Big rocks

A common analogy for prioritising is to compare different tasks to different-sized rocks, pebbles and sand. The most important things are your big rocks, and the least important things are the sand. In between are pebbles and small rocks. The different-sized rocks represent tasks of varying degrees of importance.

Using this analogy, imagine you have a bucket in which to fit all your rocks (the bucket represents the 24 hours of time we have each day); if you start filling the bucket with the sand, followed by the pebbles, then the small rocks and finally the big rocks, inevitably the big rocks won't fit in.

If we reverse the order and put the big rocks in first, we find they fit in easily. Then as we put each of the successively smaller rocks into the bucket, they fall into the cracks left by the larger rocks before them, Right up to the sand, which of course fills any gaps left. When done this way, all the rocks fit without a problem. If you do an internet video search on big rocks exercise, you'll find videos that show exactly what I'm talking about.

And so, the same goes for our business and life. If we don't prioritise the most important tasks, they simply won't fit into our day. Yet, when we do prioritise them and allocate time to them first, all the other stuff somehow still fits in.

There are several challenges most people face in following this practice. Let's go through and identify them and give you some ways to overcome them.

1. *The big rocks don't always have an immediate pay-off.* This means dedicating time to them does not feel fruitful, and we would rather be doing something that *feels* productive. A strategy to overcome this requires some future thinking. Cast your mind forward enough to get the feeling you will have in the future when the effort of this big rock task is paying off. Getting that feeling now by

thinking about the future helps to raise the importance of that task in this present moment. When you can *feel* the result of your efforts, it helps to 'justify' dedicating the time now.

I've had to use this strategy many times while writing this book. The times when I know I should be sitting down to write, the payoff for dedicating the time seems so far in the distance I would much rather be doing something more immediate, like responding to the emails I know are building up in my inbox. In these moments, I shift my focus to the feeling of what it will be like when the book is published, and the feeling of having a more concise toolbox to help my clients grow their businesses. For me, that feeling really matters and gives me the drive to dedicate the time now!

2. *You are not clear what your big rocks are.* This is usually a result of poor, or no, planning. When we don't plan or don't have concrete goals, it becomes very hard to access the level of importance of one activity over another. Refer to the section in First Principles, Planning brings clarity, and the section Planning.

If it's more of a case that you just have too many priorities or big rocks to work on, then you might benefit from the brain dump exercise we'll be covering next. And I would still suggest that a well-thought-out plan will avoid this pitfall.

3. *Lack of weekly and daily planning.* It's one thing to have overall goals, and even a detailed 90-day plan, but if you dive into your day or week without a plan of how and when

you are going to get your big rocks done, they will invariably not get done. The notion of 'I'll work it out as I go' doesn't always have a high success rate. Following this philosophy is pretty much setting you up for failure. We'll cover how to overcome this one under Default calendar.

4. *Not knowing how to get started.* You might be clear on what your big rocks are − and even set the time aside to get them done − but if you don't know how to get started, it's amazing the things you can find that need doing instead. Think back to a time when you've procrastinated on something, then finally the pressure to get it done became so great you simply had to get it done. And once you got into it − I call it breaking the surface tension − you found it really wasn't that difficult. Commonly, we create scenarios in our mind that lead us to believe a task is going to be more difficult than it really is. Breaking the surface tension of water allows things to enter the water much more easily. It's the same for each task that has a high level of perceived difficulty. These tasks have a level of surface tension that can be broken simply by taking the first step. You don't need to know all the steps to get something done, just the first one. And when you take the first step, suddenly the second and third steps become clear, and eventually, the whole path. It's like going to the gym. You might say, 'I don't know what I'm going to do once I get there.' But just by getting there you put yourself in a different environment (think back to First Principle, Your environment matters), which influences your thinking. Before long you've completed a workout you didn't know existed 60 minutes ago.

5. *The timing isn't right.* A close cousin to the previous point is the thought that you just need a few more things to fall into line, and then the timing will be right to do it. This one comes into play usually when there is an opportunity to be seized or a difficult choice to be made. The reality is, there is no perfect timing. The best analogy I've heard for this concept is that of the mother duck. Imagine if mother duck said, 'I'll start walking once all my baby chicks are lined up one behind the other.' She would never move. The baby chicks get lined up once the mother duck starts moving. We need to start moving for things to line up.

Knowing – and being able to execute on – your big rocks is *the most important* time management principle. Putting first things first is a well-known game changer. In fact, if I had to pick one differentiating factor between those who make it and those who don't in terms of getting stuff done, this would be it.

Okay, enough of looking at the traps related to making appropriate time choices. Now let's look at some tools and strategies you can use to make good time choices. Each of these can be used in isolation or in conjunction with each other. Personally, I use them all and find them critical to being effective (not just efficient).

The brain dump

To be able to execute well at any given moment requires clear thinking. One of the most common reasons we don't have a clear mind is because we are using too much of it for remembering a to-do list.

There is possibly no greater waste of brainpower than remembering to-dos. And the result of having your mind full is often feeling overwhelmed and stressed. When you keep to-do items in your mind, it can be very hard to assess and prioritise them. And when another one of those things pops into your mind, it just gets added to the pile. All you really know is they are things that need to get done, and you have not yet done them. Just knowing this creates pressure that you don't need.

When a situation arises, or an opportunity presents itself, you need to have the headspace to think about it clearly and process the opportunity. If your brain is full of to-dos, you just might not have the room. The result is anxiety and stress and no ability for creative thinking and problem solving.

Much of what follows (as with many parts of this book) has already been expounded by others. This stuff is not rocket science, yet it's amazing how many people don't practise and control these basics and subsequently operate at less than full throttle. Let's look at the steps involved in the brain dump:

1. *Get it on paper.* A brain dump is exactly what it sounds like. It's taking a blank piece of paper and literally dumping (writing) down all the things you have in your mind at that moment. The time it may take to do this will vary depending on your situation, but it rarely takes more than 3 to 7 minutes.

It's important to note that your goal is to get *everything* out of your head, regardless of whether it's work related or not. You want all to-dos, ideas and issues to pour out of your brain and onto paper. It's also important not to pass any judgement on the things you are writing down. Passing judgement is done in the next step; doing so now just distracts you from the true task at hand – clearing your brain. Having things on paper does two things:

- it clears your mind
- it makes all those things you've written down tangible, so you can see them more objectively. When your mind is crowded, it can be very hard to see things clearly, no matter how simple they may be. Having them on paper gives you distance from them and allows you to see them as independent items rather than seeing them as a part of you or your mind.

Once you've got everything out of your head, there are a few steps to follow. Exactly how many of these you do and to what level of detail will depend on what is on the paper in front of you and how you feel about it.

The end goal is to have the feeling of a clear mind and a sense of control over your situation. When you feel in control, your actions and behaviour will be more decisive. You will have a greater level of confidence and be able to make better decisions.

2. *Prioritise.* Looking down your list, move through each item and label it as an A, B, C, D or E.

- A = Important but not urgent – these are your big rock items as discussed previously.
- B = Urgent and important – these are items that absolutely must get done. The consequences of not doing so will have a significant impact on the achievement of your goals.
- C = Nice to get done – these might be ideas to improve

your business, which, while they are clever ideas, are not critical to do now.

- D = Delegate – there will be items on your list that you know immediately should be on someone else's list.
- E = Eliminate – because you didn't pass judgement as you were writing, you can now go back and look more critically at each item. There will be some you can just cross off. When you first start doing this exercise, you may not find any 'E' items. But as your awareness increases around your big rocks and how valuable your time is, the Es will come to light more easily. Always think of the true consequences of not doing a task and be aware of your mind's default nature to think of worst case outcomes. Not finding the absolute best price for your stationery is not going make or break your business, and there is little doubt you could better invest the time.

Once you've gone through and allocated an A, B, C, D or E to each item, you can go through and prioritise with numbers – 1, 2, 3 and so on. The numbers represent the order in which you are going to attack your list. You may not always need to do the numbering part of the exercise. It will depend on how clear you are when you look at all your As, Bs and Cs.

Once you've gone to the level of detail needed, you have a game plan for the day.

As you sit and look at your plan, you will either have the feeling of control and 'I can do that', or you'll look at it and ask, 'How the hell am I going to get all that done?' If your response is the latter, you need to follow these next steps.

3. *Allocate time.* Looking at the As and Bs on your list, allocate how much time you think each one needs. It should go without saying that we can safely ignore items labelled C to E because they either aren't important right now or don't require your time to get them done.

As you total the time you've estimated, again, you'll either have the feeling of do-ability or not. If the feeling is still that you can't get it all done, you now need to brainstorm a little further. Here are some questions to help.

- Who can I ask for further help?
- Who can I outsource this to?
- What are the true consequences of not getting this done?
- What questions would I have to ask of those who are relying on these actions to establish further true consequences or options for getting them done?
- How can I break down this task into smaller chunks that, if only a few were completed, would be adequate for now?

(*Note*: it can be a good idea to move your Cs off your current list to a list I call the parking lot. The parking lot is where I keep all my ideas that, while good, don't fit into the immediate or current 90-day plan. When I am sitting down to do my next 90-day plan, I'll refer to the parking lot to see if anything there is now a fit.)

4. *Execute in sequence.* Once you have your running order (ie your priority list), pick the first priority on your list and work on it until it's done. Never jump to another priority.

If you get interrupted, once the interruption is dealt with, go back to the priority you were working on. Sticking with one thing brings a level of efficiency that is unattainable when multitasking. Multitasking is a fallacy. If you doubt this, drop me an email (jamie@salesup.com.au) with the subject line 'Send me the multitasking test' and I'll give you an exercise that will prove it to you.

During the day, other things will no doubt come up that must be slotted in. Depending on how full your day feels, follow a similar process for these new items as we've covered already. Make sure you add new things to your list rather than keeping them in your head, regardless of how small they may seem. Always keep in mind that your mind is for strategic and creative thinking, not for remembering to-dos.

Default calendar

A default calendar is a graphical illustration of what your ideal week would look like if you could plan it perfectly. When you look at all the tasks you need to do in a typical week and categorise them (eg sales and business development, client service, finance and admin, team coaching, planning etc), how much time would you allocate for each and when would you plan on doing them?

Figure 15 (following) is a sample of how it might look.

Doing this exercise forces you to think about how your time would best be spent in an ideal world. Now, your actual week rarely works out as ideal, but I can guarantee you, if you plan your week with a picture of your default calendar in front of you, your actual week will look a whole lot closer to your ideal than if you were to plan it without seeing what your ideal week should look like in the first place.

Time/Period	MON	TUES	WED	THU	FRI
	Team meetings / Prep week	Working IN business	Marketing	Team meetings	Admin
				Marketing	Planning next week
					Working ON business
	Working IN business		Working IN business		
		Working ON business			
			Education	Working IN business	Education
		Client prep / misc	Exercise		
	Exercise				Exercise

FIGURE 15: DEFAULT CALENDAR

Knowing your ideal week helps you make better choices. If you know in your ideal week you should be spending 8 hours on business development, it becomes very revealing if you look at your actual week and you have only allotted 2 hours to it. It gives you a virtual reality check.

The default calendar also helps when setting appointments with others. If someone asks for some of your time this week, you can better assess the impact of your week by saying yes or no. If you are already behind on some of your big rocks, it becomes clear and easy to suggest a time the following week that suits you better and allows you to stay on track. You'll be amazed that when you become more assertive about how you choose to spend your time, most people will fall in line with your needs, simply because they are not clear on their own needs.

Once you have your default calendar, you are able to plan your week proactively. At the end or beginning of each week (my preferred time is a Sunday afternoon – you'll know what works best for you), sit down with your actual calendar and plan your week. Of course, do this with your default calendar next to you for reference. This doesn't need to take a lot of time. I generally have it done in less than 15 minutes. The weekly planning process considers the following items:

- your 90-day plan
- your default calendar
- your major priorities for the week ahead (big rocks)
- personal commitments.

When you see conflicts between what you would like to happen (ideal) and what needs to happen, you then invest some time juggling until your actual upcoming week looks as close as possible to your ideal. Some weeks will look better than others. You will know if you are straying too far from ideal for too many weeks in a row. If you are unable to allocate time for your big rock items too many days or weeks in a row, this is your signal that something needs to change.

Also, be aware that as your business grows, your default calendar will likely change with it. You'll start delegating more and be able to spend more time in areas that will become increasingly important, such as coaching your team.

A fun exercise can be to map out a default calendar on how you want your week to look in 12 months' time. Perhaps you've got some things you currently do that you really don't want to be doing, and likewise, some things you'd like to be spending more time doing. Mapping this out leverages the First Principle See your vision and gives you something tangible to work toward. It also makes the gap between where you want to be investing your time and where you currently are investing your time crystal clear. That can help you to see what you need to be delegating and in what order.

What does your business need to look like to get to this point? Who else needs to be on your team? How much do you need to grow to be able to afford those people?

For a blank template of a default calendar, log on to our resource section.
jumpingoffthewheel.com

Time blocking

This strategy goes hand in hand with the big rocks and default calendar. The concept here is to allocate 60- to 90-minute chunks of time to get your project-style big rocks done. The actual execution of this, rather than the scheduling, is usually the stumbling block for most people, so here are a few tips to help.

- Let others know your plan so they can help. These may be those who are also most likely to interrupt you.
- Set your environment for success:
  - be distraction free (no email or social media alerts).
  - if possible, disconnect from the internet – this will obviously be task dependent (there is software that can help here – search for it).
  - be out of the office. (I have written most of this book in my car sitting somewhere in nature disconnected from the internet. For me, my office has an association with client service and business development – more immediate-style activities.)
  - set yourself a reward or punishment (depending on what you respond to best) for completion or non-completion.
- utilise some form of public accountability.
- refer to the First Principle, see your vision.

How you choose to use your time is possibly the number 1 determining factor in your level of success. It has been said we all have 24 hours in a day, but the difference between those who are successful in business and those who are not is largely because of the choices that are made about how to use those 24 hours.

For more books on time choices, download our recommended reading list.
jumpingoffthewheel.com

ROLES AND RESPONSIBILITIES

While this section seems to be just another section among many, it is one area of growing your company that I've seen produce meaningful results. Those results are things like:

- less stress and a happier team
- fewer errors through better communication
- less conflict (eliminates the 'I thought you did that' or the 'That's not my job' conversations)
- happier customers (they know who to speak to about what).

I often see clients who think it is clear who does what and downplay this area of building their business. When looking at error rates, the common thinking is 'That is just how it is' or 'I don't see how clearer roles are going to fix that.'

The reality is that any time a person is not clear on the way forward or what is expected of them, there is a level of reservation or hesitancy about the way they act. Just like if you needed to run from A to B but could not see that path, there is no way you would be running as fast as you can. (Refer to the First Principle, Planning brings clarity.)

It is the same with roles and responsibilities. It's not just the individual's role that needs to be clear; they also need to understand how what they do fits into the bigger picture. The importance of understanding what everyone else around them is doing, what they can rely on others for and how the people around them are relying on them to do their part well cannot be understated.

Typically, as your company grows, the need to review roles will be an ongoing process. What works well at one level of growth is quickly outdated at another level. You may find that the way you've structured things was based on some assumptions that, it only becomes clear after implementation, were not the best way forward.

An example of this is a client we work with who had some aggressive growth targets. They were not the strongest in sales and believed they needed to hire business development managers (BDMs) to go out and drum up new business. Only after several hires did they realise this was not the right strategy for them. To execute this strategy, they had structured the appropriate support people around the BDMs. As they shifted away from the BDM model, the support roles also had to change to optimise the new workflow.

Let's borrow an analogy from sport. In a sports team, it's critical that each player knows what is expected of them and how their role fits with the other players on the team. Take rugby, for instance. In a line out, if the team doesn't know who is jumping or lifting and where the ball is to be thrown once it has been captured, it would be a disaster. Everyone needs to know what their role is and where they fit into the team. When each position on the team is filled and each player is performing their agreed-upon responsibilities, the team performs well.

It is the same in business – each position on the team serves a role. When all those roles are filled and performing well, the business performs well.

So how do we get to the point of all positions being filled and performing well? I'm glad you asked! There are three essential steps to follow:

1. map out which roles you have/need in the organisation (your organisational chart)
2. be clear on what each of these roles needs to deliver on (ie the key outcomes they need to produce – position contracts)
3. determine who the best person is for each role (role allocation).

Step 1: Your organisational chart

This does not need to be too complicated, and in fact, it should not be complicated. The more simple you keep this map, the more easily it will be understood by everyone. Our goal is to end up with a chart that maps out all the roles in the organisation.

Figure 16 is a simple template that will apply to most companies. You will probably need to flesh this out further, but it serves as a good starting point.

Notice there are no names in this figure. Your first step is to simply map out the roles as they ideally would be to have your company running as efficiently as possible. Think about this as if you were starting from scratch. What would the perfect structure be?

Resist the temptation to map out the roles based on the people you already have in your company. This will come later. If you think about your current people, it will likely bias your thinking in a way that does not create the ideal picture for your company. The picture you are going to create should be based on ideals. Once you have that, you can then start to look at who should be in which boxes and where the gaps may be in terms of number of people or abilities of your current team.

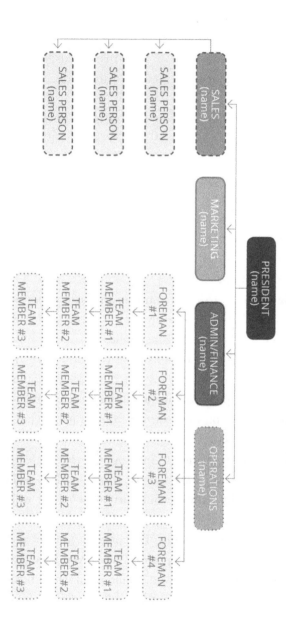

FIGURE 16: SAMPLE ORGANISATIONAL CHART

Be sure to include areas that currently are not being covered by someone. For many businesses, these are areas such as marketing or HR.

If you are a business with a small team, it can be easy to think this section does not apply to you. That is usually a mistake. Even with small numbers of people working together, responsibilities can quickly become clouded, and any lack of clarity that exists regarding who does what will lead to inefficiency, confusion and a lack of accountability.

Note: download an organisation chart template from our resource section on the website.
jumpingoffthewheel.com

Step 2: Position contracts

A position contract is a simple document that outlines the results each role is responsible for producing and details how success will be measured. It may also include key skills required and to whom they are accountable.

Position contracts are not job descriptions. I'm not a fan of job descriptions. They are usually just an extensive list of tasks a person is to perform. Rather than thinking about the tasks, get people thinking about outcomes and results they need to produce. For example, you can tell someone, 'Your job is to sweep the floor' or you can say, 'You are responsible for making sure the floor is clean.' A floor can be swept and still be dirty. But a clean floor is a measurable outcome – either it's clean or it's not. You should be less concerned with how it gets cleaned, so long as it gets cleaned.

For a position contract template and how-to guide, log in to our
resource section on the website.
jumpingoffthewheel.com

Step 3: Filling the role with fit

Odds are that you have already got someone in most of the
roles you identify in your organisational chart. Where this
is the case, you need to ask yourself, 'Is this the best person for this role and do they have the skill set and abilities
to perform successfully?' If your answer is 'yes' and 'yes',
that's great! You just need to have a conversation with the
person about the position contract to ensure everyone is on
the same page.

If your answer is, 'This is not the best person for the
role', your options are to:

- find someone who is better suited for the role
- develop a plan (with the individual) to fill the knowledge gap and bring the person's skills up to the level
  required (see the Progress and plan section).

Warning: you only want to commit to developing a person for a role if they are excited (and committed) to doing
it. Also, consider if they have the underlying talent to be
successful. By underlying talent I mean a person's natural
abilities. Some of us are better at connecting and supporting
others, some are better at logistics and organisation, some
are great at seeing the big picture and creating concepts,
some are better at the details and critical thinking. My point
is that you want to place your people in roles that play to their

natural abilities and strengths and set them up for success.

There are, of course, exceptions to this piece of advice. If you have a small team, you probably won't have the luxury of perfectly matching talents to roles because so much needs to be done by so few. This is okay. Just be mindful that when someone is accountable for a role they may not be perfectly suited to, it will require more effort on their behalf, and the results produced may not be world class. This is the real world, and sometimes we must be okay with things not being perfect. (In fact, if you want to get things done, you need to be alright with things not being perfect – by this, I do not intend that not being perfect is a licence to not do our best.)

When it comes to the implementation of position contracts and communication of your org chart, there are a few things to keep in mind.

- Depending on your culture, you may encounter some resistance. People may interpret this initiative as criticism of what they've been doing. Also, keep in mind that it's common for people to feel threatened by the change, so your positioning and communication needs to be intentional and well crafted.
- The communication needs to very clear as to *why* you are making these changes. Clear and unambiguous roles and responsibilities:
  - provide clarity on roles
  - minimise confusion
  - allow the organisation to operate more efficiently
  - provide clearer lines of communication
  - allow everyone to feel more successful in their role
  - provide a happier workplace.

- You may determine this initially as a team, then with each person to discuss how it affects them individually.
- Be willing to collaborate on this exercise. In fact, this should be your default way to move forward with the whole thing. Your team will have some important insights, and it would be wise to heed them.
- Be sure to listen to each person as you discuss their role. Be on the lookout for non-verbal signs of confusion or fear, such as silence, withdrawal or disengagement. It is important each person embraces the changes and genuinely sees them as a positive move for them and the company.
- Check in regularly and individually with your team. Change often takes time to be accepted. Your role is to keep communicating the changes and benefits. For more, see The 4 Ps of people.

WORKFLOW MAPS, SYSTEMS AND PROCESSES

Going hand in hand with your org chart is your workflow map and the systems within it. Your org chart shows who does what from the perspective of roles, and your workflow map shows the overall process of how things get done.

Workflow is essentially the path or overall process a prospect follows to becoming a customer and then a repeat customer, and how all the processes required to make that happen (eg making the product, providing the service, invoicing, etc) flow and link with each other.

SAMPLE WORKFLOW

Waterproofing Company

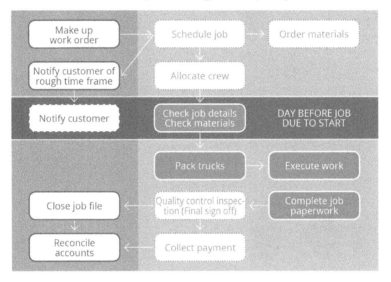

FIGURE 17: BIG PICTURE WORKFLOW

Figure 17 shows the big picture. You'll need to understand what this big picture looks like for your business, then break down each section into more detail so you can see the flow within each segment. Some of those segments may be:

- invoicing and AR management
- purchase orders, receiving and payables
- cost accounting, time sheets, and payroll
- various operation's workflows (eg how the product the customer is buying gets made and delivered)
- sales process
- marketing and remarketing flows.

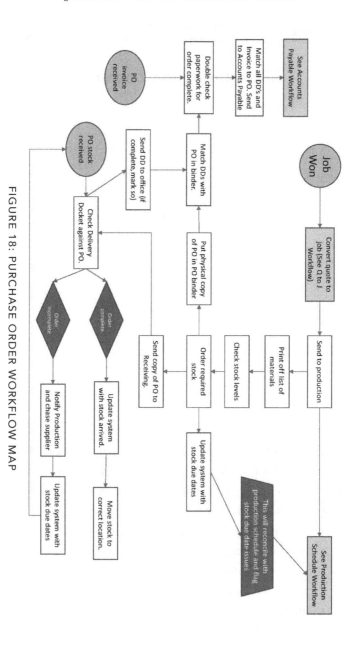

FIGURE 18: PURCHASE ORDER WORKFLOW MAP

Figure 18 is an example of a more detailed section of a workflow map for a purchase order system.

The benefit of having your workflow mapped out is all about communication. It makes sure everyone is on the same page. As your company grows, people will become more and more separated from the big picture as roles move toward specialisation rather than generalisation.

Case study: Manufacturing workflow example

Shaun and Alexis's manufacturing company had grown significantly from the early days of Shaun and his truck. It now occupied an 1800-square-metre factory and had a team of around 30 people. Shaun was trying to keep it all under control.

Among the many things we worked on to enable Shaun and Alexis to be freed from the company was getting them and their team clear on the workflow map. The way things were running, processes had grown organically within the company and no one person, apart from Shaun, really knew how things should happen. Therefore, Shaun was losing his mind.

We got the team together and walked them through how to map a workflow. In no time, they had a first draft. The exercise revealed many areas that were ripe for improvement. They started to understand why they were making mistakes in certain areas and could easily identify sections or parts of the process that needed more structure and systems.

Having it visually in front of them made it tangible. They could point to areas and communicate about what they were seeing in a way that was easily understood by everyone at the table. The old saying is true: a picture tells a thousand words.

Once they had a version they were all happy with, it was shared with the whole team. People who spent all their time in one section of the business suddenly could understand the whole business and see how what they did fitted in with the big picture. It was a game changer for engagement and discussions on how to improve.

Their workflow map is now a living document that is the starting point for any discussions on process changes and improvements.

In the early days, if it's just you and a couple of employees, it's not hard to communicate how things get done. As you grow, it's easy for people to lose sight of how the sections of the business are connected.

There are a couple of reasons why a workflow map is so beneficial.

- It provides a visual. As Shaun and Alexis discovered, once they had a picture, many things made more sense, which made them easier to discuss and communicate.

- It gives a benchmark and a standard to work from. Rather than processes being something that are only talked about and verbally communicated, mapping them defines them in a way that mitigates misunderstanding and also links processes together into an overall system.

- It exposes sections of the workflow that are not working well, or where there is confusion.

- It allows the team to work on improvements in a structured way. Sometimes too many improvements implemented without a systematic method leads to more confusion. When the workflow is mapped, improvements can be prioritised and adapted at a rate that is manageable. Specific parts of the workflow can be identified and focused on. Again, it comes back to tangibility and clarity.

Implementing a workflow

To get your workflow map in place, here are some suggested steps:

1. Get a pad of sticky notes and a blank wall or whiteboard.
2. On each sticky note, write down a step in the process.
3. Put the notes up on the wall in sequence.
4. Keep doing this, making changes and additions, until you feel you have a good starting map of the overall workflow.
5. Identify sections that need to be expanded into more detail.
6. For the sections that need more detail, follow steps 2 to 4 for each.
7. Have these drawn up in PowerPoint or similar, so they are clear and easy to read.

(*Note*: the sticky note strategy saves you from erasing and starting from scratch each time you need to make a change. It's an easy format to brainstorm in until you get a product that is pretty much right.)

Once you've got your workflow maps done, share them with the team and post the relevant sections on the wall in the appropriate departments of the business. Each department might get a copy of the overall workflow map plus the detailed version of their section of the business. For example, the admin section would get a copy of the overall map as well as the invoicing, purchase order and payroll processes.

Linking workflow maps with the org chart

Being a visual (and slightly OCD) person, I like to have the org chart and workflow maps colour coded so it's easy to see which sections of the business look after which parts of the workflow.

It's not complicated stuff and as I've already mentioned, the more visual you can make communication, the easier it is for more of your team to get it. It's one thing to talk about stuff, but for many people, seeing it can make all the difference.

What is the difference between a workflow map and a system or process?

Great question. The way we define it, a workflow map is an overall picture of how each step connects and flows. A system or process contains the specifics and detail on how each of those steps is to be done.

How do you create effective systems?

I'm not a huge fan of large operations manuals that spell out exactly how everything should be done. I get that they are good in theory; I've just never seen them maintained (things are always changing) or referred to on a regular basis.

I believe a system is something that should be integrated into the daily workflow in a way that makes using it intuitive and necessary. It is sometimes important to have things written out for reference, and from what I've seen, just having it written in a binder is a recipe for failure and non-compliance.

The simplest example of an integrated system is a checklist. Let's say that when a quote becomes an order, the details of the order are printed on a job ticket, and on this ticket are the various checkpoints that must be completed. This job ticket could physically follow the job as it moves through the various stages of production.

It does not matter whether this job ticket is a physical item or digital, but for the job to move to each stage, the previous stage checklist must be completed and signed off on. This forces the system to be used and provides the necessary double checks. It also creates accountability at each stage of the job (through the sign off).

Compare the checklist system with a binder on a shelf that people need to refer to so as to make sure things are being done properly. The binder requires conscious thought to consult and is not in someone's face. You may still have a binder that provides more detail than can feasibly be present on the checklist. However, it's not necessary to read the binder every time to be prompted on the necessary steps for the process to be successful.

In our business, we use a piece of software that allows us to create digital systems and processes that are automated or require tasks to be checked off for the next stage to be triggered. The software allocates tasks to people and tracks completion. When we have a new client come on board, the process is all mapped out, and we never miss a step because it's almost impossible to do so. The design of the system forces its users to follow the process. Figure 19 is a picture of that system – it's a little small, but you can see the labels showing some of the steps.

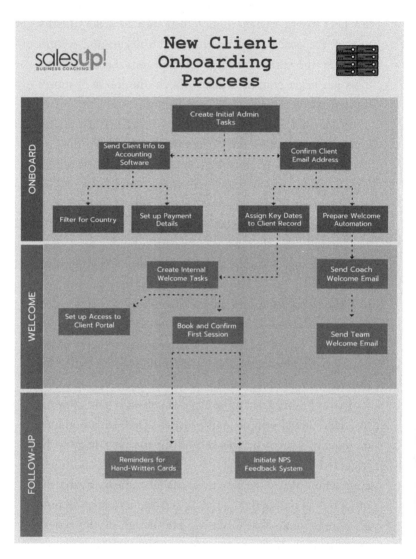

FIGURE 19: NEW CLIENT ONBOARDING PROCESS

A system should be easier to use than the process involved when it is not used. This is the art of creating a great system. Be guided by where your systems are not being followed or where errors are happening, and rather than pointing the finger at the people running the system, ask: how can we improve our system to make it easier to use?

W Edwards Deming (the father of quality) stated that 94 per cent of errors are system errors and 6 per cent are people errors. This should give you some guide on how important it is to create effective systems.

TECHNOLOGY

The previous discussion on systems design leads naturally to the topic of technology. My previous example of our own business and the use of our software shows how powerful technology can be.

Technology is a form of leverage, meaning that with the right technology solutions, you can achieve greater levels of productivity with fewer people. Not only that, but it also reduces errors (by minimising double entry or manual entries), will allow more opportunities to be realised and gives you greater transparency on what is going on in your business.

I won't be giving any specific recommendations because business needs vary based on many factors. Solutions are also changing and improving, so my recommendations would be quickly out of date. As you read through this section, just think about how well you are using technology and where there may be opportunities to better apply it to your business.

The following are just some of the key areas in which technology can give you either a distinct competitive advantage or a massive resource leverage.

- *Marketing.* The ability to use automation (eg if someone downloads something from your website, an automated action sends emails, or a task is created for someone to follow up, or the customer is added to your newsletter list) combined with analytics gives you insights that allow you to continually hone your marketing efforts, thereby increasing your marketing return on investment and effectiveness.

- *Sales.* Running an accurate and up-to-date CRM system that keeps track of customer buying patterns, prospect activity and your sales pipeline will give a real-time pulse on the key drivers that affect your revenue. You can see conversion rates at a glance, order and quote trends. If you are cloud based (as with any of the points above), it allows you to stay in touch remotely. If you have an outbound sales team, this is critical.

Case study: Technology boosts estimating efficiency

Garry and Isaac's printing business needed help. They were in a commodity-based industry in decline. They had not moved with the changes and the writing was on the wall. Something had to change.

It was clear we needed to revisit the way they were marketing the company (currently they really weren't marketing … that was just part of the problem) and that was going to take some time. We didn't have time and we desperately needed some quick wins. We needed to cut costs.

In relation to technology, we looked at analysing their estimating and quoting processes for sales. We took a quick look at some data (luckily, they did have data) and we helped them see that:

- they had several customers they were doing massive amounts of quoting for, but winning very little work from. If we stopped quoting for these customers, they would lose very little revenue but save approximately one-third of a person's time – time that could help get other quotes turned around faster. And speed was the name of the game to increase conversion.
- their costings were outdated and their quoting practices were inconsistent. This made it very hard to know which type of jobs were making money and which weren't.
- the efficiency of one of their estimators was horrendous. She was doing about 30 per cent the number of quotes of the other estimators. When they considered this, the team quickly identified a number of her methods that, with just a bit of extra training, improved her speed, again allowing for faster quoting and better conversion.

This analysis took the client about an hour to do. The payoff was increased conversion rate, more accurate and profitable pricing and time savings in the quoting team. Without the data, Gary and Isaac could never have taken these actions because they would not have known the opportunity was there. It was a small step in their turnaround, but one that was sitting there for the taking. Sometimes the simplest things are right under our noses. We just need to know where to look.

- *Communications.* Both externally (customers and suppliers) and internally with your team. Much time in business is spent communicating, whether it's finding out a delivery time for a customer or letting the sales team know about a new product. If you were to track how much time was spent by your team performing some form of communication, you would see it is an astounding amount of time. Getting streamlined here is a game changer.

Case study: Automating some customer communications

Martin's team were continually fielding calls about availability of product and delivery times (they supply and manufacture glass products all over North America). Looking at the resources required to service this need, it was clear there was opportunity.

After some research, Martin found a third-party solution that bolted on to his computer inventory system and CRM software. This solution sent out weekly notices to customers updating them on stock levels, delivery times and back orders. Their inbound calls dropped overnight to almost zero. Customers loved it.

Big win all round.

You see the kind of technology Martin installed now used all the time when you order something online. As a customer of a business that is doing it well, you are rarely left wondering what the status of your order is. And if you are wondering, there is almost always a way you can find out 24/7.

- *Business intelligence.* With the huge array, availability and affordability of business software, it's possible to know almost anything about your business at the click of a button. Gone are the days when this was a big-company-only space. The smallest of businesses can now have access to world-class software and the business intelligence that goes with it. Business intelligence is the analysis of data within your business that gives you the power to make better decisions.

  An example of business intelligence might be cross-referencing your 'marketing' expense line from your income statement to your 'number of new customers' from your CRM software to calculate a 'cost per customer' metric. Or simply reporting on your ration of new versus repeat customers over time.

  The options here are endless. You just need to work out what the critical information is for your business, then look for the solution that can provide it.

  Business intelligence may already be built into the systems you are running, or you may need to invest in software that will extract, compile, analyse and report from your software solutions.

Most software is now built with an open API architecture that allows varying levels of integration with other software. This means that unrelated software packages can speak to each other. In the earlier example regarding client onboarding in our business, our CRM software sends client information to our accounting software, so we don't need to re-enter it. This is possible because of the open API architecture.

Case study: Technology helps owner keep up with growth

Simon's manufacturing business (building products) was doing well. It was making about 13 per cent net profit and growing at approximately 30 per cent year on year. However, as his business was growing, Simon had a feeling things were getting sloppy, particularly now that he could not be involved in all areas of the business in the way he used to be.

One of our first steps was to upgrade his accounting systems. Investing in a modern cloud solution not only gave better visibility on the numbers, but also eliminated the need for one person in the office. We redirected that person to overseeing the marketing – something she was much happier doing (and better at) and that no one was currently doing.

The next step was to invest in some workflow software that would computerise the team's job management and allow them to do accurate cost accounting. When we brought this idea to their attention, they shuddered at the thought of how much work was involved.

We persisted to help them find a solution. Ninety days later they were excited by the information at their fingertips. They could now see margins by type of work, conversion rates, rework levels, and non-productive time. It gave them so much data with which to better understand their business, and the opportunities to improve were immediately clear.

Previously there was justification and hunches. Now there was clear undisputable data that gave them an objective way to have discussion about what was working and what wasn't. Game on.

PEOPLE

MY BELIEF is that business can be boiled down to two things: people and numbers. They represent the left and right brain of business. This section, of course, is dealing with the right brain – the 'people' half.

This point of view begs the question: which is more important, people or numbers? It's not an easy choice, and I'm not sure there is a clear answer because you need both. I do know, however, that getting the people side of the equation right can make the life of growing a business a lot easier. Great people have instinct, they solve problems and they are dynamic. In short, getting the people side of your business right can create magic – which in turn creates profit.

Of course, the opposite can also be true when you get the equation wrong. The people side of the business can cause massive inefficiency, stress and frustration. No one wants that, and it's not what you went into business for. Hence the need for a framework that will get the people side humming and thriving.

The following 4 Ps will be your guide to getting your dream team in place. They will help you attract and grow a team that is committed to growing a healthy, sustainable business.

(*An important note*: like every section in this book, your people strategy does not stand in isolation. Everything is connected. How you approach your people will affect your numbers and your operations. How you approach growth will affect your people, and so on and so forth.

As you read through and start to apply the strategies in this section, keep the First Principles in mind. How well you apply the First Principles will have a profound influence on your efforts to create the dream team.)

PURPOSE

If you happen to be reading this book close to the time it was published, I'll forgive you for rolling your eyes at the title 'Purpose'. It's somewhat of a buzzword at the moment, and it has become a buzzword for good reason – purpose matters.

For a person to truly be alive and fully engaged in life, they need to feel a sense of purpose. They need the sense that what they are doing has meaning and value. Purpose is the emotional fuel that helps us get out there and make things happen. Of course, motivation to make things happen can also come from necessity (everyone needs to eat), but to go beyond the 'have-to' type motivators, people need to tap into their purpose.

An individual's purpose can be anything from building

a personal fortune to solving the world's most dire social issues. It can be to raise confident children or to develop a community group focused on the elderly. There are no rules.

An individual's purpose will be guided by their values and their beliefs. The level of commitment to that purpose will also vary according to those same values and beliefs.

Now, if you're reading this and wondering what your purpose is or feeling like you should know and don't, you're not alone. Yes, ideally you should know what your purpose is, but most people don't. If you're unclear or have never thought about it, sit tight. We'll cover how to find your purpose later in this chapter.

Just as the purpose is important to people, it's also important to businesses. Businesses are living entities. Yes, there are many businesses out there that are surviving despite a lack of conscious purpose, but I challenge you to find one of those where the people are thriving.

It is absolutely essential to tap into purpose when building your dream team. Below, I'll walk you through some key points that will show you, first, why your business purpose is important and how you can make it work for you. Second, we'll explore how you might go about determining the purpose of your business.

Why is your business purpose so important?
TEAM ALIGNMENT

Your business purpose creates a common goal. Inevitably, everyone sees things differently, and in the day-to-day operations of your business it can be easy for people to be caught up in their own agendas (not always intentionally), confused about priorities or frustrated by the lack of alignment where everyone is working toward the same goal. A business purpose can serve as a centring mechanism that, when brought to the forefront, grounds the team to remind everyone why they are there.

RECRUITING

As mentioned earlier, there are individuals who are clear on their purpose, and plenty more who are not. Your company's purpose will help to attract and recruit both those types of people, and it is handy for you to understand how each will respond to your recruiting efforts.

- *Those who know their purpose.* When you talk about your purpose in your recruiting process, applicants whose personal purpose naturally aligns with your business purpose will be attracted to the role. Because it's somewhat rare for a business to be clear on why it exists, it can be an attractive quality to job seekers when a business is able to clearly communicate it in a way that has feeling and commitment.
- *Those who don't know their purpose.* Just because someone does not have or know their own purpose does not mean purpose is not important to them. It's just something they've never thought about. When you explain your business purpose to them, either it will resonate or it won't. If it does, then that person is going to be fuelled by having a purpose to rally behind. They will discover that working on purpose is so much better than going through the motions to collect their pay.

You won't need to explain the benefits of your purpose – people will just get it because that is the way we are wired.

Remember, for people to be fully alive, they need a sense of purpose. So, when you give these people a purpose worth aligning themselves to, you can give them more life. You'll help light them up.

GETTING THROUGH THE TOUGH SPOTS

I don't need to tell you that business is not always easy. If there is not some greater reason why we are doing this madness, it can be tempting to give up. The same goes for your team. If they are there just to collect their pay, when times get tough (and they will) it will be tempting for them to seek out new opportunities with perceptibly greener pastures.

When a team is dedicated to a purpose that is greater than them, quitting isn't an easy option. It would be akin to letting someone down. People whose values are aligned and who believe in the purpose their work supports don't like the idea of letting people down.

TAPPING INTO THE FULL 100 PER CENT OF TEAM POTENTIAL

There is an enormous difference between coming to work because you believe that investment of time is going to make a difference and matter in some way, and putting in the time so you can get paid.

Someone who is working just for the pay governs their effort relative to what is necessary to keep that pay coming (ie do just enough not to get fired). If you are looking for a little more than that from your team (and I certainly hope you are), then you need to offer more than just a salary.

Being clear on your business purpose does far more than just engaging your team – it engages you! If you are clear on why your business exists and the importance of the work you are doing, that is going to translate to your team, your customers and everyone else your business touches.

Your business purpose gives your business soul, which makes it stand out in the marketplace. When you consider businesses that have a soul, which businesses come to mind? It's an interesting question.

How do you find your purpose?

Before you even look at your business purpose, it helps to get clear about your own. If your purpose does not align with your business purpose, you are going to have a tough time convincing others theirs should too.

Write down the first things that come to mind when you answer the following questions.

1. What are your three strongest talents?
2. What are you doing when you are using them?
3. How do you feel when you are doing these activities?
4. What does a perfect world look like to you?

Now, looking at what you've written – and if you've written nothing, go back and do it! – see how you can connect the dots. Using the words and language from what you've written, write a phrase that says something to this effect: 'My purpose is [the activities that utilise my strongest talents] or [using your strongest talents] to have an impact on creating [your ideal world].'

Keep working at it until you come up with something that makes you tingle a bit. It doesn't need to be grandiose or use complex language. You don't need to impress anyone. It's for you and only you.

Finding your business purpose

Now you need to ask yourself, 'Why does my business exist?' You might say 'To make me money!' which may be true, but that is just a by-product of fulfilling your business purpose well and building a great business.

The other point to consider in revealing your business purpose is that it should be inspirational to you and to others. Remember, you'll be using this to align the team, attract top talent and get people through the tough times. So, a purpose based on making you money is not going to cut it, I'm afraid.

Here are the points to consider.

1. What are the three core talents or skills your company most likes to use, in the form of nouns (eg communication skills, design skills, complex manufacturing etc.)?

2. List up to three activities your company likes doing that best expresses the above skills, in the form of a word ending in 'ing' (eg designing, presenting, constructing)?

3. Describe in 10 words your company's view of an ideal world, in a sentence beginning with, 'Our ideal world is one in which ...'

4. Now, put the above work together into a statement of purpose using the structure below. This will serve as your starting point. Take some time to edit it until it feels right. It does not need to stay in the same structure. (And preferably, it won't. Avoid corporate sounding statements – make it human and colloquial).

'We will use our (list the three talents), by (list the three activities), to create a world that (write the ideal vision).'

Here are some examples to get you inspired. (You'll see how the way they are written varies massively. There are no rules – just what feels right to you.)

- Google – to organise the world's information.
- SpaceX – to revolutionise space technology and enable people to live on another planet.
- Seventh Generation (consumer goods company) – to inspire a consumer revolution that nurtures the health of the next seven generations.
- Patagonia – to build the best product, cause no unnecessary harm, use business to inspire and implement solutions to the environmental crisis.
- REA Group (Real Estate company) – to make the property process simple, efficient and stress free for people buying and selling a property.

As you look to communicate your purpose to your team, and potentially the outside world, I can't stress enough that this is not a tagline or some form of marketing spin. Yes, it may help your marketing, but that is not its primary role. It needs to come from the heart and be something that you can talk about with genuine passion, care and enthusiasm.

People need to know it is real, not just something you've thought up to impress people. People can tell the difference no matter how well you dress up the latter. When it's real, it carries energy and authenticity that can't be fabricated, which is why the essence of it is more important than the exact words. If it is taking you some time to find the right words for your purpose, that's okay. In the meantime, just talk about it in whatever language comes out. If the feeling and intent are there, the words will follow, and in time you will find the right copy that conveys it in a concise and straightforward way.

I can't stress enough that this is not a box to tick on your quest for business success. This is something that should feel like an extension of you and the things you care about.

PLAYING RULES

Playing rules refer to the standards and values of your company. They are the guidelines for how you behave as a team and what you will settle for. Your playing rules will help determine the people you will attract, the people who will stay, and in turn, the culture you foster. Your playing rules equal your company culture (if you uphold them).

This is the part where you get up on your soapbox and declare what you stand for. I say that in jest, but it's not too far from the truth.

You see, every business already has a culture, whether you are conscious of it or not. The question is, do you currently have the culture you want?

Culture design should be intentional. Perhaps you already have the culture you want, and if you do, kudos to you for instilling that in your organisation, even if by accident.

The true test of your culture is to know what happens when you are not there. A strong and healthy culture will permeate the company way beyond the influence of any one person. A weak culture that is dependent on the presence of the owner will quickly unravel upon the owner's absence.

Culture is one of the key defining factors in a company's

ability to grow. Think of company culture as you would an individual's constitution. A person with a strong constitution can endure much more pressure and force than one whose constitution is weak. As your company grows, your team will experience varying degrees (and sometimes extreme levels) of pressure. Your team's ability to handle that pressure will be greatly influenced by the strength of your culture.

Case study: The power of culture in times of tragedy

Michael and Tara's company was growing rapidly. It had reached the point where it was getting too much for them to handle, and they knew they needed to upskill. That's when they hired us.

Of the many opportunities we identified, clearly defining their playing rules was on the list. The team was growing and, unlike when it was small, some different attitudes were creeping in to the workplace, and Michael and Tara felt they were starting to lose the tight family feel.

Luckily, Michael was a very strong leader from a standards perspective. He was well respected, he cared for his team and didn't suffer fools lightly. He was firm but fair, and subsequently there was a strong culture base to build on.

After we had defined the playing rules and infused them into the company, there was a measurable difference in the way the team worked. Some people left and others stepped up. It became clear very quickly when new hires were a fit and when they weren't. The team truly embraced the concept.

Before long (after implementing some further systems and redefining some roles), it was possible for Michael and

Tara to be away from the business for extended periods of time, and when they got back, things were just as they were before they left.

Their team enjoyed telling them they'd been made redundant. And they almost had.

Then tragedy struck. Michael became critically ill, and it was clear the business needed to fully operate without both him and Tara while she cared for him. Even though the situation was extremely unfortunate, the business didn't miss a beat. Yes, there was some tweaking to do, but the team stepped up, solved any problems and adjusted to the new reality. Michael's essence, represented by the core values he'd instilled in the company, shone through loud and clear. The playing rules are clearly in the DNA of the company – it's who they are as a team.

Contrary to Michael and Tara's story, I've got too many examples of companies whose playing rules are either non-existent or meaningless. The tell-tale signs of this can be high levels of absenteeism, difficulty finding good people, low morale, high staff turnover and general lack of mojo among the team. I'm sure I don't need to point out why these symptoms are problematic for growth.

So, how do you go about getting your playing rules in place? Do you just sit down, write out what comes to mind and the next morning declare them from the stage, Jerry Maguire style? Or should it be a little more structured and strategic? To be honest, it can be either. The first step, though, is defining your playing rules, so let's look at how you do that.

Defining your playing rules

Think about it this way – you've got a set of values (things that are important to you) that make up who you are. Some of those values are specific to business in general and some apply to life in general. Similarly, each of your team has values in the same way. What we want to do is distil the most important and relevant values/rules that you and your best people live by, and articulate them in a way that represents what makes your team what it is (or perhaps should be). There are really two approaches to getting this done.

1. *Have the leadership do it*. That may be just you or you and your key people.
2. *Get more of the team involved*. This is potentially a sampling of people from each department right through to involving the whole team.

The path you choose is up to you, and I've successfully used both approaches with clients.

If you choose to do it with just you or you and your leadership, it will be faster and you'll get exactly what you want, but the possible downside is you may not capture something that is important to the team, and more importantly, you may not get the full buy-in and ownership that is critical for your team.

Some of the situations that warrant input from leadership alone are:

- the culture is already strong, healthy and clear. Putting it on paper is more of a formality than a brand new initiative.
- the culture is toxic. You need to get it right so you can create change. Getting others involved will open a

can of worms and take you down an undesirable path. (*Note*: correcting this type of situation requires a few more steps than just documenting your playing rules.)

On the flip side, if you get the team involved, it's more likely there will be higher levels of buy-in, but it can take longer and it may not always represent 100 per cent of what you want.

If given a choice, I do prefer getting the team involved for a few reasons.

1. The buy-in factor. If someone doesn't feel ownership around something, it just never means as much, and that gets reflected in their behaviour.
2. The process makes it really clear who should be on the team and who should not. When we've done this exercise on team days, those who aren't aligned clearly stand out. More on how to deal with that later.
3. Good people have similar values and they want to see similar things in the company's playing rules. In the many times I've done this exercise with clients, there are always similar themes that come out. So, the fear of ending up with something you don't want is remote.

Once you've decided on the right path for you, the next step is how to draw out your playing rules. Here are some questions that can help flush them out.

- If you were to ask your very best people, 'What are the values most important to you that make you who you are?', what would they say?
- If you were on-boarding someone during their first day of working for your company, how would you

guide them in their behaviour so they would be the perfect employee?

- If you were coaching your child (if you don't have one, pretend) about how to behave at the playground, what would come to mind?
- What thoughts do you want your customers to have after dealing with your company? How would your team need to act to leave that impression? What values would guide those actions?
- When your people are asked by their friends outside of work, 'What is it like to work at [your company]?', how would you want them to respond? How would your team need to think and act for your people to feel that way? What are the underlying values that would guide that behaviour?
- If you were to look at some of your C and D players (see the Dealing with C and D players section), what is it about their behaviour that is lacking? What values might be missing there?
- For your company to be a leader in its field, what sort of team would you need to have? What standards would that team strive to live up to?

(*Warning*: some of these questions will lead you to define aspirational-type answers, ie what you would like to be rather than what you are? That is fine as long as it's not too far from where you are now. When you define your playing rules, everyone needs to feel they are a true representation of the team. If the rules appear to define something you are not, they will lack power. Your values must ring true. You'll be able to feel it when it's right.)

How many playing rules should you have? There are no right answers, but I've seen it work best when there are less rather than more. You want them to be easy for people to remember, so if there are 17 of them, well, that might be a tad much.

A general guide would be to have 3 to 5 playing rules.

How you write them matters. If you use generic terms like respect, honesty or teamwork, you might find it helpful to add some explanation to these words that reflect your company's DNA. Generic words tend to sound very vanilla, and consequently, elicit a lacklustre response from your team.

When your team read the playing rules, you want them to know that these come from your company. Ensure they have character and feel. Here's an example.

Case study: Unique playing rules

When we began working with Simon, he wanted some help with his team. During our conversations, it became clear his people problems were due, in part, to unclear expectations being set by him. Simon needed playing rules.

Simon's first attempt certainly got the ball moving in the right direction, but it lacked the punch that helped Simon and the team feel ownership. Here was his first attempt.

Ownership – taking ownership of the company and customer success.

Perhaps you can see the essence he was aiming for here, but also see its vanilla flavour. When he went back to his best people to ask them how to better phrase the concept he wanted to communicate, this is what they came up with.

You eat what you kill.

Harsh? Perhaps, but work a day in their company and you'll soon pick up the intensity of the team. This playing rule makes it very clear that if you don't perform, you don't stay. Those who do stay love it because everyone is alike and thrives on performing.

If you do an internet search on company culture or core values, you'll get lots of examples that can give you ideas. One company that has been well documented is Zappos in Las Vegas. Investor turned CEO Tony Hsieh took the lessons he'd learned from growing his first companies, and the cultural disasters they'd become, to form a very intentional (and well-documented) culture that was exactly what he wanted.

In his book, *Delivering Happiness*, you'll find the tactics and strategies the company used to achieve this. Some creative practices include paying people a significant lump sum of cash to leave during their orientation and having the team write a culture book each year that describes how the culture affects them. Zappos has become the poster child for modern-day company culture (at least at the time of writing).

The culture of your company will have a massive impact on the happiness and performance of your team. If you've got a small team, it's far easier to breed the right culture through your own leadership actions. As the team grows, you have less ability to influence each person, not only because there are more people for you to affect, but because others in your company are also influencing them.

The goal in developing your playing rules, and hence defining your culture, is to have everyone influencing one another the same way in terms of values and behaviour choices.

Bringing your playing rules alive

It's one thing to define your playing rules, but making them real, keeping them alive and embedding them deep in the organisation is another. You don't want to be one of those companies that proudly has the playing rules or core values mounted beautifully on the wall, but no one knows what they are.

Developing your playing rules is not a one-off exercise that allows you to tick off a box and then move onto the next thing. It's an ongoing commitment and a critical part of your leadership. So, here are a few ideas for implementing, embedding and maintaining momentum:

- Be sure your playing rules are part of your recruitment and on-boarding processes.
- Build stories (real ones) about the company that exemplify the playing rules in action. People love stories, and remarkable stories get passed on. For example, think of times when the team went way beyond, took some risks and just blew the client's mind.
- Celebrate actions that are in alignment with the playing rules.
- Bring attention to the playing rules through internal communications (emails, newsletters, internal documents).
- Openly talk about the playing rules at meetings (both departmental and company-wide).

- Put them up on the wall or around the workplace (see the First Principle Your environment matters).

There will be times when your commitment to the playing rules gets tested, you want to let some behaviour slide or a difficult choice needs to be made. These are the golden moments that really bring your playing rules alive. Accepting the temptation to take the easy choice is a downward spiral and lets the team know the rules are negotiable. Don't do it.

Even if you think no one will find out about your choice, your commitment and persistence in maintaining the standards is the core driving force behind them. Never waver, regardless of any perceived negative impact. Those perceived outcomes are always either only short-term or just don't eventuate.

We see this most often when there is a reluctance to deal with people on the team who are highly skilled but won't come around to living the playing rules. (We call these people C players – see the Dealing with C and D players section.) The fear of the gap they will leave in the organisation if they left can be paralysing. The reality is, if they are no longer there, you'll work out a way to get the job done without them. The rest of the team will step up, or you'll find a replacement more easily than you thought you would, or you'll even realise they weren't as good as you thought they were. We've seen this play out so many times, and can say with certainty, it's never as bad as it appears it might be.

Case study: Standing up for the playing rules

Matt was a brilliant chef and ran a very popular and successful restaurant. One of his main challenges, however, was some turmoil among the team. It was affecting the customer experience and people were starting to make comments to him. It needed to be addressed.

We pulled the team together for a team alignment day. During that day, one of the things we talked about was the kind of environment they wanted to work in. As with most people, they were looking for a place that was fun, supportive, had good people to work with and where they were challenged and acknowledged for the excellent work they did. In our experience, these kinds of themes are very common. Through this discussion the team established their playing rules.

During this process, it was clear that not *all* the team were on board with it. Nancy (the highest-performing server by average sales volumes – she was brilliant at the upsell – by quite a margin) was giving all the body language of, 'This is a bunch of BS. I'd rather be anywhere than here with these people.' Matt saw it too, as much as he didn't want to.

The day ended with a real sense of alignment. The team (mostly) were thrilled to have some clear ground rules and expectations on how things were going to be moving forward. I warned Matt that he was about to be tested on the work they had done. He knew what I meant and was nervous. It was clear Nancy was not on board, yet Matt really didn't want to lose her selling power. It was a real dilemma for him. I reiterated to him the importance of sticking to the standards. He promised me he would.

Sure enough, it was not long before Nancy's behaviour toward the rest of the team continued and needed to be addressed. As hard as it was for him, Matt stepped up to the task, and addressed the behaviour. The difference this time was he had some objective benchmarks (the playing rules) to show Nancy where she wasn't living up to the standards they'd agreed on.

This went on for perhaps 3 weeks before she threw in the towel (literally) and left in a rage. Matt was shaking, but the rest of the team breathed a sigh of relief.

And you might be able to guess what happened to the performance of the remaining team. Yep, it went up. And it went up beyond what was necessary to make up for the loss of Nancy's sales.

You might argue that was the long way around in dealing with Nancy. And it may well have been. But now the team had a clear set of standards to operate by, and more importantly, Matt had the tools to make sure he only brings on the right kind of people moving forward. He also has an objective reference to address behavioural issues should they arise again.

Sometimes, the long way is the short way.

PROGRESS AND PLAN

To grow a business, you need to grow the people within it, because the people are the business. People affect the customer experience, develop and execute the systems that facilitate growth and shape and execute the marketing. Overall, it is largely the actions taken by the people within your business (including you) that determine the numbers you see on your financials.

The concept of progress is part of growing your people. It is providing ongoing regular feedback to your team so they know if they are on track or need to make changes.

Unfortunately, this is an area that is common for business owners to avoid, and from what I've seen, such avoidance happens for a few reasons.

- You've got more important things to do (in your mind).
- You're not sure what to say.
- Things are going well, so there really is not much to say.
- You're afraid of the possible confrontation.
- You're afraid of being asked for a pay rise.

These are all valid thoughts. However, they don't excuse you from checking in on your team and giving them the feedback that they deserve, and frankly, want.

We all like to know if we are on track. In fact, if we are not quite clear on where we stand, we won't put our full effort into moving forward, and there will be a level of trepidation. It's like driving a car. If you are unsure of what is around the corner, you will proceed with caution. However, if you know what is around the corner and are confident of your abilities, you can take the corner at speed. You want your team to move forward with confidence and certainty – and of course, with enthusiasm.

So, how do you provide feedback on a person's progress? It's really a simple conversation. Think of feedback in terms of coaching, not critiquing. Your goal as a leader is to develop people and to help them grow. This needs to be the foundation from which you operate. When you do, and your people understand this, the coaching and feedback process will flow smoothly. No one likes to be critiqued, however well people thrive on personal growth and coaching.

Traditionally, we are advised to give annual reviews. This is typically a formal session where you sit down with the employee and give them feedback on where they are doing well, on where they need to improve and on pay levels. While I believe this can have value, I don't think it's the starting point for most people, particularly if you aren't doing any kind of review right now.

The two key issues that are usually covered in a review are pay and performance. I think it's better to separate these two items and discuss them independently. Good performance does not automatically mean someone gets more pay, just as a pay rise doesn't just hinge on performance. While there is a link between the two, that link is not always linear and straightforward. For this reason, we are going to discuss them separately here.

Let's start with performance. I believe performance can be measured against two things:

1. behaviour
2. results.

Both are important, and one is not more important than the other. Behaviour can be measured by whether the job is being done in a way that is consistent with the playing rules of the business (ie are you a good person to work with or not?). Results are self-explanatory and can be summed up by whether the job is being done successfully.

Each coaching session may not always contain both

elements. Each has a time and place for discussion.

Factoring in some of the topics we've already covered, discussing performance becomes much easier when you've got a clearly laid out position contract and have your playing rules established. Having both of these in writing gives you clear objective standards by which a person's performance can be measured. Without these, you run the risk of being perceived (and possibly being) subjective and judgemental, which is not a good start to fostering a person's development.

Coaching your team

Every day, opportunities arise to coach and provide feedback. Never wait until an annual review – discuss the subject at the moment it occurs or very soon after that. Think of it this way: when you do sit down for your annual review, nothing you ever say should be a surprise. Everything you cover should already be on each other's radar; the review is more about documenting progress and agreeing upon action steps to move forward.

A coaching session may be off-the-cuff as the opportunity arises or you might set up a more structured ongoing schedule if you both see a need for closer support. Often, it will be a combination of the two.

Where you set up a more formal coaching structure, always be clear about the objective. Sure, you will have some general how's-it-going?-type conversations, but there should ideally be a measurable goal the player is looking to achieve (ie becoming more assertive with clients or improved accuracy in estimating).

Regardless of the format, the key to coaching is to ask

questions. Resist the temptation to be instructional by telling them what they need to be doing. That said, there will be times when the person being coached has no idea how to move forward and may need some direct instruction, but most of the time they already have the answers, they just don't have the questions that will unlock them. Your goal in coaching someone is to change the way they think. This is done mostly through questions. For example, John is having trouble getting longer lead times with customers. He feels the pressure to say yes and please them, but it is having a detrimental effect on production with tight delivery times. Your questioning might go something like this:

- Q: John, when a client asks you about delivery times, what is the first thought that pops into your head? (It's even better if you can use an actual client's name to make it more real for John.)
- Q: What are the consequences to our production team when we accept tight deadlines? And how does that affect you? How does that affect our other customers?

After teaching John that the First Principle of win/win is thinking, you may ask:

- Q: John, could you relay that principle back to me in the context of how we balance our customer's needs with our own?
- Q: When you are interacting with a customer, what would be useful for you to remember to help increase your assertiveness around lead times? How could you make that happen? What support do you need there?
- Q: What techniques or what things could you say or ask to help find a win/win time frame with a customer?

(This is testing for knowledge and helping John think through the best way for *him* to change.)

• Q: Sometimes to change our belief about the way things are, we need some evidence to help us believe it. One way to do that with minimal risk is to do a test. Which client do you think you could test out your new methods on just to see how they work? How might you go about that?

When you ask your employees questions, you actively engage *their* brain, not *yours*, to find the answer. When your team is better at finding their own answers, their abilities and confidence grow. And they will ask you fewer questions, making them more autonomous, leading to things getting done faster.

The review

So yes, I do believe in reviews annually (or even bi-annually). In-the-moment coaching is great, but it pays to support it with a level of structure that centres everyone and allows everyone to be really clear on all that has been discussed.

The format is simple. Prior to the meeting, you and the employee individually fill out the Feed Forward form (see below), giving your thoughts on where things are at for that person. Then you come together to review and discuss. Throughout the discussion, you'll both establish what the path needs to look like over the next 6 to 12 months and document it, and that will become your plan for the ongoing coaching until the next review.

If you are uncomfortable with these kinds of discussions, I have two tips for you.

1. Review some of our First Principles, particularly Radical responsibility and Pressure is your friend. It also really helps if the employee understands these principles too.
2. As mentioned, read *Crucial Conversations* by Kerry Patterson, Joseph Grenny, Ron McMillan and Al Switzler. It is a terrific book, and a real game changer for having conversations that might become difficult.

THE FEED FORWARD FORM

The Feed Forward form, a term borrowed from Jack Welch, is quite straightforward. It simply takes the content from your playing rules and the position contract and applies a rating scale to allow both you and the employee to allocate a rating based on how you each see it. The form is shown in Figure 20.

There is no right or wrong in terms of how the rating is done. The rating process is simply a way for both parties to express how they see things. It's a more measured way of defining your views. When there are discrepancies between your rating and the employee's rating, a discussion is required.

You may not always get to a point where you both agree, and that is okay. From your position as the leader, this gives you an insight into the way the person thinks and how it is different from your own. You need to decide how big an issue the discrepancy is, and what you need to do about it. To go further on this subject is really the content of another book, so we'll leave it there for now.

The outcome of completing and discussing the results of the Feed Forward form should be points for the individual to work on. If someone thinks there is nothing to work on, that is usually a red flag and should be kept in mind.

On the flip side, you don't want too many things to work on as this can be overwhelming and counterproductive. I suggest limiting it to a maximum of three things. If there are more than three, pick the top three and make the duration before the next Feed Forward session shorter than you might otherwise have done. Many clients have used a 30- or 90-day increment, depending on the need.

If a person is in a new role and needs more support and guidance, you might use a shorter time frame. There really are no rules. You need to judge each situation on its merits and make a decision that feels appropriate.

At the end of each session, both people get a copy of the finished Feed Forward form (which now contains each person's ratings as well as the agreed upon actions) and you set a date for the next session. And that's it. Done!

The plan

As much as people like feedback on how they are doing, they also like to know where they are going. There are two areas where you may want to think about bringing some clarity and direction to your team.

1. Company plan and direction – what are the company's goals, how are we going to get there and what is everyone's role in making that happen?
2. Individual plan:
    i. short term – what is my immediate coaching/development plan?
    ii. long term – what does my future look like? Where can I advance?

FEED**FORWARD** >>

Player: ____________________ Coach/Leader: ____________________

Position: ____________________ Others in Attendance: ____________________

Date ____________________ ____________________

SCORING REFERENCE 1=NOT GOOD 2= NEEDS ATTENTION 3= JUST OK 4= GOOD 5= OUTSTANDING

PLAYING RULES	PLAYER	LEADER	ACTIONS
1			
2			
3			
4			
5			

ROLE ACCOUNTABILITIES	PLAYER	LEADER	ACTIONS
1			
2			
3			
4			
5			

PLAYER GOALS (PERSONAL)	PLAYER GOALS (PROFESSIONAL)
1	
2	
3	
4	

Signed: ____________________ ____________________

Player *Leader*

FIGURE 20: FEED FORWARD FORM

Some of these items are not new to us by this stage of the book, and some are, so let's dive in and take a closer look at each.

COMPANY PLAN

We've already discussed this in significant detail in First Principles See your vision and Operations/Planning. It is about having a pretty good idea of where you want to take the company in terms of direction and goals. You may not always have a clear idea of how you are going to make this happen, but knowing the direction is important. For a refresher or more information, refer to those previous sections in the book.

The key point here really is about the sharing of the vision and the plans behind them. It's much easier not to share your goals because you won't look foolish if you don't hit them. The challenge with that is it's very hard to get a team aligned and excited to grow if they don't understand where they are headed. If you don't know where you are going or are not excited about where you are going, then you have little motivation to act.

When I've coached clients through this topic, I explain to them that you don't need to present your vision and goals to the team like Leonardo DiCaprio does in *The Wolf of Wall Street*, making a declaration to his office. It's okay not to be 100 per cent clear on the details. Quite often, once you've got a general idea of your direction, the details come. Your team will likely have inputs and ideas that can help as well.

When you are discussing this with your team, be open and genuine about where you are in terms of the level of clarity. That said, if you really are not clear on where you are going, I'd suggest putting some time into that first. Don't approach your team and say, 'I have no idea on where we are going.' That is not very inspiring.

The worst thing you can do is say nothing. I can pretty much guarantee, people who work at companies that have no communicated vision, goals or direction, are not fully engaged. They just turn up to their job to collect their pay. Maybe they have good friends who work there, and people are nice, but it will be a status-quo environment.

If you were to give those same people the opportunity to be part of a company that is going somewhere, has a healthy culture and develops its people, it won't be a competition as to where they would rather work.

Hopefully, you are starting to get an idea of why direction, goals and a plan are important. This becomes particularly important and powerful when we start to look at recruitment.

INDIVIDUAL PLAN

The two levels of the individual plan are:
1. short-term coaching and development
2. longer-term future with the company.

We have already covered the short term in the Progress section, specifically with the outcome of the Feed Forward form. Developing some habits and routines in having these conversations with your team will put you in decent shape here.

The longer term is also straightforward. It's just about asking your people where they see themselves in the future. It is good for you also to have an idea of where you see them. Here's an example of how this went recently for one of my clients when they sat down to have a check-in with one of their key people, who ran one of the sections of the company:

Owner: *Hey John, we just wanted to check in to see how things are with you – get some feedback on some of the changes we've been making and generally get a feel for where things are at from your perspective. (This is how the meeting was positioned. John is a long-term, loyal employee who started at the company straight out of school. John is reserved, so getting him one-on-one is crucial for him feeling safe to speak up.)*

John: *Thanks. Yeah, things are pretty good. We've been super busy but generally no complaints.*

Owner: *That's great. Look, we're really pleased with how you are running things in your department. And I know with things being so busy, sometimes we don't always get a chance to look at the bigger picture or check in personally with how things are for you.*

John: *Sure, no problem.*

Owner: *How are things going with your team? (The conversation continues, discussing different individuals' performance, team culture and general operational ups and downs.)*

Owner: *John, how are you doing? Where can we offer more support for you?*

John: *Yeah, I'm pretty good. Like I said, it's been busy, which has gotten a bit stressful at times, but all in all things are okay.*

Owner: *Sure. I can see that. And John, how do you feel about your role? You've been looking after that section for several years now, and doing an excellent job as I've said. What do you see for yourself in the future?*

John: *(in a shy manner) Funny you ask. You know how you are thinking about putting on another site supervisor, well I would be keen to have a crack at that.*

Owner: *(Surprised, as he was not expecting that response.) Wow … really. Okay, well, that's great. I'm really pleased you spoke up about that. I would not have guessed it. How long have you been thinking about that?*

It turns out this was a perfect move for the owner. It was much better to have someone they knew to head out on site rather than an unknown new person. However, prior to that conversation, all focus was on hiring someone new. When I asked my client why they had not considered John previously, their response was, 'I just never would have thought he'd be interested.'

Lesson: never assume you know what people want, and always provide the forum to allow them to share their goals and desires with you. Be genuinely interested in your team's future and check in with them on a regular basis.

When people know you care about them and their future, they reciprocate and care about you and your company. Caring is not only good leadership practice, it's also good human practice.

PLAYER RECRUITMENT

It cannot be stressed enough – if there is one most important aspect of growing a business, it would be getting great people on board. Great people do great work. Great people come up with creative ideas. Great people attract other great people. Great people don't create political environments. Great people deliver results.

So, recruiting is massively important, but this is an area in which many owners underinvest in terms of time, effort and money. Before we get into the recruitment system, we must discuss a few things that need to be in place to be able to attract great people.

First, you need to have a strong vision and purpose – and you need to be excited about it. It's tough to get others excited if you are not. And it's tough to get people inspired if there is no clear direction or purpose. Great people want to be working toward a vision that matters. (Refer to the Purpose section.)

Second, your culture (refer to the Playing rules section) will attract or repel great people. It is important to have done some work here because your playing rules will be an important component in the recruiting process. It is also important for those playing rules to be alive and well within your business. The culture of your business has energy. That energy needs to be strong, vibrant and healthy.

Third, involve the necessary people in the selection process. Heads of departments and co-workers should all play a part in recruiting. Allow them to interact with the people who will form part of their team. Doing so will result in better results, more accountability for team selections and less turnover overall which is great for business.

Fourth, recruit ahead of time. When you are proactive, you are in a mindset of control and patience rather than feeling overwhelmed and rushed. Too many businesses leave hiring to the last minute. They exceed their current capacity in work volume and then rush to get someone in to help with the excess work. A rushed hire rarely works out well.

Fifth, always be hiring – even when you're not. Good talent is rarely sitting there waiting for your ad to run. The best people are already engaged and working somewhere. You want to have a pool of people you are courting and building relationships with, so when the time comes to hire, you're not starting cold. The A player you are looking for might be someone you meet at a social function, it might be the guy at the supermarket checkout, it might be the sales person working for your competition. Always be on the lookout.

Sixth, be human and be real. On the other end of your hiring process are people with aspirations, fears, feelings and families. In this hiring process, you are going to talk to a lot of people. Your hiring process should reflect your company. Craft all your steps and communication in alignment with these thoughts.

Now, with those ground rules out of the way, let's look at how to hire.

Hiring should be a process. A process that can be run by almost anyone in your organisation and a process that gives you consistent results.

Most of the time, when people follow their gut when hiring, it backfires. That said, I've worked with a couple of unusual clients who really did have a knack for picking good people. My experience tells me they are the exception to the rule, and we don't want to base your success on following the exception. So, let's look at the player selection system.

The system

The key philosophy behind this system is de-selection. The idea is to attract as many applicants as possible, then allow them to de-select themselves based on the barriers you are going to put in their way. It is also important for your mindset to be one of de-selection. You want to be in the mindset that if you don't find the ideal candidate, you won't hire in this round.

There is nothing worse than feeling like you *have* to hire. That is when the big hiring mistakes are made. Think back to our ground rule of 'recruit ahead of time'.

If a candidate gets the feeling that you are extremely selective, it brings exclusiveness to the process. We don't do this with a fake-it type of approach. It must be sincere. I truly want you to have a selective mentality.

Picture your current team like a finely balanced mix of chemicals that, if they were to tip slightly off balance, would explode. Your job as the chemist is to test all new chemicals you want to add to the existing mixture to make sure they are not going make an explosion. You must be selective or your business will be blown to pieces (or slowly incinerated from the inside).

STEP 1 – YOUR IDEAL CANDIDATE

Define your ideal candidate. This step might seem quite straightforward, yet the more detail you can define, the more chance you have of finding the ideal person. There is an attraction process that helps here (like in all areas of life).

The clearer you are about what you want, the more chance there is of you getting it. The main purpose of clearly defining the ideal candidate is:

- you can then write the best advertisement – one that is going to stand out and be noticed (see Step 2).
- as you are reviewing the candidates through the process, the ones who are the closest match to your ideal will be obvious. This will make selection easier.

Download our ideal candidate profile to help you here
jumpingoffthewheel.com.

There is an assessment for the ideal candidate profile called DiSC. DiSC is a framework for identifying and understanding behavioural styles. There are many other systems out there, such as Myers–Briggs and Colours, which essentially provide the same information. DiSC just happens to be one that we've used extensively.

Understanding behavioural styles is a quick and easy way to determine who will be the ideal fit for the role. To help you along, here is a summary of the four behavioural styles.

(*Note*: for each of the styles, the strengths and limitations are preceded with the words probable and possible. This is because, in reality, each profile will consist of a mix of each quadrant style. No one behavioural style falls solely within one quadrant. The exact mix will determine which strengths and limitations are most prominent. Regardless, the list below gives you a good snapshot of how each style presents itself.)

1. *D – Driver* (not to be confused with the driver in our three levels of growth)

   Probable strengths:
   - results-oriented
   - fast decision maker
   - takes action
   - big-picture thinker.

   Possible limitations:
   - dismissive of the input of others
   - lacks empathy
   - values results over people; can tend to forget about the team
   - impatient
   - can anger quickly.

2. *I – Influencer*

   Probable strengths:
   - socially and verbally firm
   - very optimistic
   - good at persuading people
   - can see the big dream and communicate it
   - people-oriented
   - team-oriented
   - motivated by praise and positive comments.

   Possible limitations:
   - acts impulsively – heart over mind
   - unrealistic in appraising people
   - inattentive to detail
   - situational listener
   - disorganised.

3. *S – Steady*

Probable strengths:
- loyal to those they identify with
- good listener
- patient and empathetic
- likes to have a team environment
- long service is deemed important
- oriented toward family activities
- motivated toward traditional procedures.

Possible limitations:
- tends to get in a rut
- maintains status quo
- resists change
- holds grudges
- lacks projected sense of urgency
- slow to act without precedent
- hesitates to move
- may do work themselves and not delegate.

4. *C – Compliant*

Probable strengths:
- critical thinker
- high standards for self and subordinates
- well disciplined
- maintains high standards
- motivated by the right way to proceed
- accurate.

Possible limitations:
- leans on supervisor
- hesitates to act without precedent

- bound by procedures and methods
- will not risk starting new ideas without a qualifying statement
- does not verbalise feelings
- may do work themself and not delegate
- yields position to avoid controversy.

STEP 2 – WRITING YOUR AD

Writing a powerful ad (like any marketing) is only possible when you know who you are writing it for; hence the importance of knowing your ideal candidate. It's important to use words in your ad that are going to be attractive to the person you want.

WANTED
Fun-loving, professional, open-minded, wannabe ROCK STAR physiotherapist

If you are looking for an environment where you can unleash your talents and operate with a team that supports you toward your professional goals, then we want to meet you. We are a unique style of clinic looking for a unique style of therapist.

Please email applications to careers@physio.com and experience our unique approach to hiring.

For example, if you are looking to hire an admin person and you want them to be conscientious, detail-oriented, quiet and analytical, you start with something like: 'Seeking (insert job title here). An important position has opened up for a responsible, detail-oriented, analytical thinker who thrives on getting things right.' You would not use words like 'fun', 'creative', 'driven' and so on.

Opposite's a short-form example that worked very well for a physiotherapy clinic we worked with.

Does that look like most of the ads you see out there? No! It's different and attention grabbing, and knowing the type of person the client was looking for, it worked perfectly.

A different example is this long-form ad we used to find our marketing and PR manager.

World Class Marketing and PR Manager

Good news! We are hiring – and we are bloody excited about it!

We are a small team with a big mission, and we need someone (hopefully you) to help us kick it into a higher gear. First, you need to know what we are all about – read on and we can tell you about the superstar we are looking for and the role you'll be responsible for.

What we do
The work we do matters.

In short, that work is helping business owners play a bigger game, build great businesses and do it all without sacrificing their life for it. Another way of looking at it is: we grow business owners who in turn grow great companies.

Great companies are growth-oriented, profitable, have great people, have strong and healthy cultures, and add value back to society in a way that makes the world a better place.

That might sound a little altruistic, but we don't care, it's what we do, and we know it matters.

Our company is growing, and we need to add to the team to keep our momentum going – that's where you may come in.

Working with us

We are a core team of two, with two others supporting us in contracting roles, and we are spread all over the world. With that said, I (Jamie and owner of the company) am in Pottsville, NSW, and would prefer you to be somewhat local.

We are a highly autonomous team who take our work seriously, but don't take ourselves too seriously. We look after each other, and we do what it takes to get the job done. On the flip side, we all have interests outside of work and understand the value of balance.

We rely heavily on technology. We use Google Apps, Slack, Trello, CRM and all sorts of other cool toys that allow for better workflow. You need to be comfortable (and competent) with all that; otherwise, you may as well move on to the next ad ☺

We invest in ourselves. One of our core values is responsibility. We believe we are the creators of our results (all of them, not just the good ones), so we work on ourselves to become better and become more. That is a cornerstone and non-negotiable.

While we work to a plan, we are far from perfect. We, meaning I, often take on too much and have been known to change focus too often. These are constraints we are aware of and are committed to working on. Be prepared.

About you

You are a person who thrives on making things happen. You are strategic and intentional. Once you are clear on the direction to take, you pursue it with dogged tenacity. You are an influencer and persuader and love to chase down an opportunity.

You are a strong communicator who is very comfortable picking up the phone and building rapport with clients, alliance partners and prospects. You are versatile and responsive and are not fazed by a random curve ball.

You have a history in marketing and sales (in professional services preferably), and you understand the balance between building a brand and generating measurable results.

People enjoy being around you because of your charismatic, caring and positive nature. You like to have fun and are supported by a strong social network.

Your role
You will be the lead creator and owner of our marketing plan and calendar. You will be responsible for its execution, measurement and results.

Your activities will vary from, but not be limited to, creating and issuing press releases, sourcing speaking opportunities, managing our social media presence, developing and maintaining alliance partnerships and leading direct-mail campaigns. You will always be on the lookout for opportunities we can leverage to gain marketing exposure.

You may help oversee and manage the initial stages of our sales process. You will be responsible for keeping our database current and ensuring we nurture our contacts as appropriate.

Initially, the role requires four days per week. It may change depending on your needs and ours.

Your typical week will be 70 per cent following a plan and 30 per cent responding to current conditions – whatever they may be.

You will be working mostly autonomously. We are a very flexible company and focus on output vs input. While we have an office presence in Kingscliff, NSW, we (I) am rarely there. I work where I am, which can be anywhere.

How this will work once you are on-board, we can discuss further.

Next steps

So, you're still reading – that can only mean one of two things:

1. You're reading for amusement, but there is no way you're going to apply. In that case, I'm glad we've entertained you, and maybe you know someone else who *is* a good fit?

2. You feel this role could be the one for you. If that's you, here's what you need to do. We'd like you to tell us a bit about you – and not through your CV. Sure, you can include your CV if you like, but we'd like to know the real you and why you think you were made for this role. You can present that information however you feel is appropriate for the role.

Email your application to careers@salesup.com.au, and from there you'll hear about the next steps. Thanks for applying and we look forward to connecting with you soon.

We supplemented this ad with a video that was posted alongside it. It worked amazingly well, attracting some top applications. (*Note*: at the time, our business was located in an area that is considered regional, an area that many would [and still do] say is hard to find good talent in.)

We've had many clients change their ad format to mirror the one above with consistent results.

STEP 3 – CAST A WIDE NET

In today's world of recruiting, there are so many places to advertise, from traditional newspapers to using your current employees' social media and everything in between. It can pay to think a little creatively here; for example, the local community noticeboard, church bulletin, school newsletters and so on.

Remember, our goal here is to get as many applications as possible. Now, this may freak you out a bit, and you may be wondering, 'How am I going to sort through all the resumes?', but don't worry about that at this stage. That comes in the next step.

A common mistake I see people making is assuming a potential advertising avenue is not applicable to the type of person they are looking to hire. For example, if you are looking for a CFO, you might think that advertising on a free website would be a waste of time. And you might be right, *but* I have seen some amazing leads come from the most unexpected sources.

My belief is that you should advertise wherever you can. You just never know where someone might be looking or perhaps where your ideal candidate's friends might be looking. Of course, you want to include the obvious channels for a role, just don't limit it to them.

A key point here is to make sure you get the applications to come in by email to an email address unique to the ad you're running. Don't use your own email address or you will get overwhelmed rapidly. See the next step.

STEP 4 – EMAIL AUTORESPONDER

Now that your applicants have applied by email, you need to set up an autoresponder to send a reply to each applicant. That reply is going to be asking them to call a phone number and answer a few questions. If you would like a copy of that script, check out the resources section on our website (jumpingoffthewheel.com)

The benefits of getting people to call a phone number and leave a message are many.

1. It will filter out those who have applied without sincerity. It's common for people just to fire off applications and resumes en masse, going for the shotgun approach. If you start your process by looking at applications and resumes, not only are you investing time reviewing probably unsuitable candidates, you need to know how to filter them out. This step will do that for you because, guaranteed, these people won't complete this step.

2. It will filter out those who can't be bothered taking this step. And if they can't be bothered doing that, what else can't they be bothered doing?

3. It may get them to move out of their comfort zone, which is something we are going to get them to do as much as possible because we like people who will do that.

4. It saves you a lot of time. Do not look at any resumes before the applicants have left a message.

5. You get to hear how well they follow instructions (based on the email script).

6. You get to hear how they sound. Did they prepare? Were they smiling? How creative were they? Did it sound like they have the mojo you are looking for?

Now, obviously, if you are going to have people call and leave a message, you need to have a number for them to call and the answering machine set. Some options include:

- a spare extension on your phone system (if you have one)

- your regular phone number, but get them to call after hours
- a spare mobile phone
- a virtual phone mailbox (there are plenty of these services around – Google it).

Make sure you check how long a left message can be and indicate that in your email instructions.

STEP 5 – CREATE YOUR SHORTLIST

As people leave a message, you need to score them. Figure 21 shows a sample scoring sheet.

This step is simple – you are looking for the best responses that are a match for what you are looking for. So, again, be clear on what you are looking for.

The best responses are not necessarily the ones that are best presented (unless you are hiring for a position where presentation is key). Back to our admin example, someone who is polished might be overkill for the position. Someone who is a little nervous, stutters a bit but seems to be real and genuine could be a great fit.

STEP 6 – THE TEST DRIVE

The next step is to take your shortlist and give them some short projects that will allow you to see them in action.

When selecting new people for your team, the two main criteria you are looking for are attitude and skills. With regard to attitude, you'll be assessing that all the way through this process. With regard to skill, that one can be a little harder. Most people just wait till the person is in the role to see what they can do. While that is certainly one way of

PHONE
RESPONSE
SCORING
SHEET

 Candidate name

 Phone number

 Call details

Time: _____ AM / PM

Date: _____

 FIRST Impression (Circle)

1 2 3 4 5 6 7 8 9 10

Classification:
(circle one)
D   I   S   C

V   A   K

salesup!
BUSINESS COACHING

RESPONSES

Question #1
_____
_____
_____

Question #2
_____
_____
_____

Question #3
_____
_____
_____

Question #4
_____
_____
_____

Question #5
_____
_____
_____

Question #6
_____
_____
_____

 THE FINAL WORD

Was this person smiling?   Y / N

Final impression? (circle)   1 2 3 4 5 6 7 8 9 10

Proceed to next round?   Y / N

FIGURE 21: PHONE RESPONSE SCORING SHEET

doing it, it also requires a level of commitment from both parties, and if things don't go well, it ends in a bit of a lose/lose outcome. The now-unsuccessful applicant needs to look for another opportunity (having potentially just left gainful employment) and you need to start your process all over again. You might be able to approach the other candidates from the recent recruitment effort, but they may also have taken other positions.

Our way around this conundrum is to give the applicants a chance to showcase their abilities through a test drive. We suggest being very upfront about what you are doing. Generally speaking, people are willing to invest some time to make sure a hire will result in a good match for both parties.

The test drive is about creating some scenarios that will simulate the role and represent some real-life situations in which you would need the new hire to perform well.

Crafting these scenarios can be fun and may require a little creativity, depending on the role. Think about the key skills required for the role. What are the skills that will enable the person in that role to do the job well and add value to your company?

Let's look at some examples. For our marketing and PR manager role, we identified the three core areas we were looking for competency in:

1. ability to plan and execute on a marketing plan
2. ability to generate PR
3. social media savvy.

Given these three areas, we crafted three scenarios (one for each competency) that would give us insight into each applicant's thought process and skill set. (*Note*: sometimes the thought process is more important than pure skills. If someone does not have the required skill or experience, but does have the underlying thought process to be able to develop the skill, that is something to consider. For example, they may not have experience running a social media campaign, but if they understand what is important and why, they will stand a good chance of being successful at it.)

The scenarios were:

1. Develop a draft 6-month marketing plan and calendar for SalesUp! Business Coaching.
2. Write a press release from the following brief (we provided the brief).
3. Describe how you would go about developing a social media presence for SalesUp! Business Coaching.

As you can imagine, the responses to these scenarios gave us great insight into each applicant's abilities – way more than an interview alone could do. We got to see how much detail they went into and their level of understanding, as well as their computer skills in presenting the information.

Here is another example. A client of ours in Canada needed to hire a sales person who would be responsible for generating new accounts and managing existing accounts in the space of customised manufacturing.

The three core areas were:

1. relationship management including balancing the needs of the business and the customer
2. new customer acquisition
3. technical abilities – being able to take the customer brief and communicate it clearly to engineering so they could provide a quote.

The scenarios were as follows:

1. Outline your plan for the first 90 days in the role. What will be important? How will you structure your time? Show us a draft of your plan.

2. A significant client that we have been counting on to reach our sales targets has fallen off. Our sales numbers are now trending down 30 per cent. How would you go about bridging this gap? What steps would you take?

3. A project you have been working on with a relatively new client has not met their expectations. They have the potential to be a significant long-term customer. How would you approach this problem? What would be your ideal outcome?

4. You're on site for a client who wants a quote for a quality control workstation:
   - it needs to be height adjustable.
   - they require overhead lighting and a lower shelf for storage.
   - draw a sketch of this workstation that you could give to engineering along with a bill of materials.

Another example is a client who owns a window washing company. The client had applicants write out step by step how they would wash a car. This exercise gave the client insight into the applicant's logic and detail orientation, which were both critical to the role.

A client in the PR field conducted mock client engagement sessions via video conference where she got to see the candidate in action, and then had the applicants write a follow-up brief.

In all these examples, three things are achieved:

JUMPING OFF *the* HAMSTER WHEEL

1. You get to see how the applicant thinks.
2. You get to see their skills in action.
3. They get to experience what the role will be like.

Before you send out the test drive, there is one very important consideration. You are about to ask a potentially important hire to make a significant investment in time and effort – perhaps more than they have done in any other hiring to date. Therefore, it's critical they feel strongly about being successful in this application or else you may lose good applicants at this stage in the process.

You cannot make people excited about the role and your company, but you can communicate all about it and give the applicants the opportunity to make *themselves* excited by it. This is where your vision, goals, purpose and playing rules come into their element. The intangible aspects of your business are the elements that will inspire and elicit passion and excitement in those who resonate with your message.

Find the right channel to communicate this message. This will vary depending on your style. For us, video is a great fit. It allows us to communicate the message with emotion. For others, it may be the written word. Just be sure that it's presented in a format and with the level of care that convey authenticity and all the passion you feel. This communication is about transferring energy and emotion.

Regarding the timing of this message in the context of the test drive, I recommend sending them at the same time, saying something along the lines of the following.

Congratulations! We loved your message and would like to learn some more about you. The next step is going to require some time investment on your behalf and will give you some deeper insights into the role you are applying for. It will also give us a chance to see how you think and help us assess your skill for the role.

Before we ask you to do this though, we've taken the time to tell you a little more about us (actually a lot more), so you can be sure this is a role you feel excited about. If after watching/reading/ listening to what we have to say, you don't think this is the right role or company for you, that is totally fine, and we thank you for your participation so far.

On the flip side, if our message further confirms you are in the right place, then please proceed to complete the accompanying scenarios. We are really excited to get to know you more. Thanks again and we'll speak soon.

STEP 7 – RESUME AND ASSESSMENTS

From the results of the test drive, you are going to have a few top picks. From here, you are going to do the following.

- Ask for a copy of their resume (at this point it's worth investing the time to look at this in detail).
- If you have not already, have the candidate complete a DiSC (or similar) profile.
- Use a tool such as the Flippen Profile. This profiling tool is the Rolls Royce of assessments and enables you to see what someone is really made of. It's impossible to fake as it uses a 360-degree approach (the underlying algorithm is mind blowing), and tells you where someone is going to excel and struggle in the role. You can then tailor your interview questions to target those areas and see how they respond.
- One-on-one interviews. Now that you have the best

candidates and some assessment information, you can have a meaningful, behavioural-based interview. This means asking, 'Tell me about a time when …' or 'Here is situation X … how would you handle it?' questions rather than 'yes/no' questions.

- References. I believe it's worth calling some referees, and I think the best question to ask is, 'If you had to start again, would you rehire X?' In their answer, you are looking for length of pause, and tone, not necessarily what their words are (though they obviously do matter).

This last step is quite a bit more involved than the length of its description may imply. The art of interviewing is a deep topic and diving into it is beyond the scope of this book. If this is an area you would like to learn more about, check out my recommended reading list (jumpingoff thewheel.com).

For a list of interview questions, visit the resource section of our website.
jumpingoffthewheel.com

That pretty much sums up the system we've been refining for the past 15 years. It has had massive success for the clients we work with. And while it may seem like a lot, once you understand the underlying principles and you have the basic framework in place, it's easy to run.

I cannot stress enough the importance of tailoring this to fit your organisation. What I have outlined is a bare bones framework. Run it like this once, then examine how well it worked for you and make changes as necessary. Like any system in your business, it will need ongoing refinement and tweaking to get the most out of it.

Best of luck and may you attract the most awesome rock stars to your business!

Dealing with C and D players

Having an effective recruitment process is critical for getting the right sort of people, but what if you have some people right now who you would rather not have? This is a good question and one worthy of discussion.

When it comes to thinking about the quality and fit of people in your company, skills and attitude are the two key components. For the purpose of this discussion, let's map these two components on a chart and then we can look at where the various levels of 'fit' fall.

On Figure 22, you can see we've plotted A, B, C and D class people.

The As are your rock stars. You want more of them. Give them what they need, including coaching and room to run, and they will do wonderful things.

Your Bs are the puppy dogs. They are keen and have the right attitude but need training. And that's okay because they are eager for it.

Your Cs are your proverbial pot-stirrers. They get the job done and many times do it well, but they have a level of toxicity. They stir things up, may think they are better than others and generally are not dedicated to playing as a team. You'll find a different variation on this theme, but you know who they are.

Your Ds are just dead weight. They really should not be on the team. Both you and they know it's not the right fit, but no one has had the guts to do anything about it.

(*Note*: when it comes to recruiting, you are looking for As and Bs.)

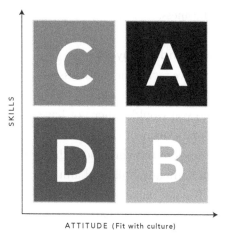

ATTITUDE (Fit with culture)

FIGURE 22: SKILLS/ATTITUDE MATRIX

WHAT DO YOU DO WITH THE CS AND DS AND HOW IMPORTANT IS THAT?

First, let's deal with how important this is. It is critical. You won't attract or retain As and Bs if you've got Cs and Ds on your team. And if you do manage to attract them, their performance will never be what it could if the Cs and Ds were not there. End of story.

Now, let's discuss what to do about it. The first step is to look at you and your leadership. I've seen many situations where the leader's view of the individual was as a C player, but when questioned about playing rules, role descriptions, coaching and leadership, there was lots of room for improvement in how this was handled at an organisational level. I'm not saying you must have things perfect, but if someone is not clear on expectations, it's hard to say how that may play out in their behaviour.

I've also seen situations where it was simply a personality style clash, and when everyone was educated on styles and how they affect communication and understanding, there was a new perspective created that completely changed the dynamic.

Again, without knowing the specifics of the situation, it's impossible to prescribe the correct course of action. I'm just saying, before you point the finger at any person, spend a moment reflecting on the many things we've covered so far in this book and ask yourself where you may be contributing to the situation. What could you do differently in the way you lead that could be the first step? (See First Principle, Radical responsibility.)

The most common factor that creates tension is unclear expectations – expectations around employee roles, outcomes and playing rules. If these are all clear and the person is still not coming on-board, it's time to start applying more pressure. Pressure will make change happen. It has to. (See First Principle, Pressure is your friend.)

Pressure is applied by addressing their behaviour and performance in the context of the clear expectations you've both agreed upon (see Roles and responsibilities and Playing rules). Either the person will come on-board or they will leave. I'm not saying this will be easy or without turmoil, but don't avoid it for fear of either of those two things. Keep applying pressure until change happens. Be sure to document all discussions, as required by any employment legislation in your country or state. In most cases, using the Feed Forward system (signed by both parties) will work, but get professional advice on this.

The long-term benefits of having A and B players far outweigh any short-term pain of helping someone move on. The reality is, if you are unhappy with them on the team, others are also, including the person themselves. Most often, people find change hard and will rather stay in a tricky situation than take a chance on an unknown situation – better the devil you know. Don't settle for that. It's up to you to make change happen.

If you've got reservations about doing this, revisit First Principle, See your vision. Remember what you are working toward. Are you going to let others deter you from achieving it?

BRINGING IT ALL TOGETHER

BUILDING AND GROWING a great business is not an easy task, which is why most people are not successful at it. With that said, most people don't have the knowledge or tools that have been outlined in this book.

Even with all the knowledge (and obviously there is more to know than has been covered here), it's still a massive challenge. That is where the gold lies. The true value of building a great business is not the end result of having a great business, but it's who you become – someone who is able to build a great business.

It's my belief that the emotional rewards far outweigh the material rewards. In the end, the only reason we want material rewards is to satisfy or create an emotion anyway.

If you look at all the areas of your business I've covered in this book, it can be hard to know where to start. I'm going to take a couple of lines here to address that.

First, there is no right order. There are no sequential steps that will make it all work perfectly for you. Compare it to learning at school. Is it more important to learn English, Maths or Science first? You need all of them, but you'll progress in each of them as you are ready, or the need arises; not necessarily in a pre-determined order.

There may be many areas of your business that can benefit from using some of the tools and approaches covered in this book, but there will be one or two that stand out more than the others. There will be a couple of areas that either you have a greater interest in (be careful not to avoid a critical issue just because it's not interesting to you) or you just know are the ones that will get you on the right path or give you the biggest bang for your buck.

You also have the decision trees at the beginning of this book as a reference. Use those to guide you, not only in which parts of the book to read, but also in what areas to work on improving first.

Building a business is a journey, and one that is never finished – unless you sell it, of course. As you work on different areas of your business, you may feel you've developed a level of mastery, only to find some time down the track you need to revisit one area again because things have changed, or the business now needs a different approach, or the larger team you now have has unique needs. It's an organic, evolving process.

I've tried many times to develop a cookie cutter approach that gives a step-by-step guide to building businesses and have not yet managed to do it. And the more I try, the more I believe that it's not the way it should be.

It's about knowing where you want to go (vision) and knowing the first few steps. As you take those, the next steps will become clear, and so on.

So, start with your vision and pick a few first steps. Now get started. Good luck.

TOOLS AND RESOURCES

SECTION	TOOL
MONEY	
Cash flow	1. Understanding financial statements
	2. Cash flow forecast tool
Investing	3. Recommended reading list
GROWTH	
Marketing blueprint	4. Ideal customer profile tool
	5. USP tool
6-point model	6. Blank 6-point model
	7. Retention rate calculator
	8. Marketing vehicle checklist
	9. SA wheel
	10. Pricing – increasing vs discounting
Planning	11. 90-day plan
	12. One-page sales plan

SECTION	TOOL
OPERATIONS	
Time choices	13. Default diary template
Roles and responsibilities	14. A guide to writing position contracts
	15. Organisational chart
PEOPLE	
Progress and plan	16. Feed Forward form
Player selection	17. Ideal candidate profile
	18. Phone response scoring sheet
	19. List of interview questions